DK WORKBOOKS

6th Grade

Geography

Author Ira Wolfman

Educational Consultant Gary Werner

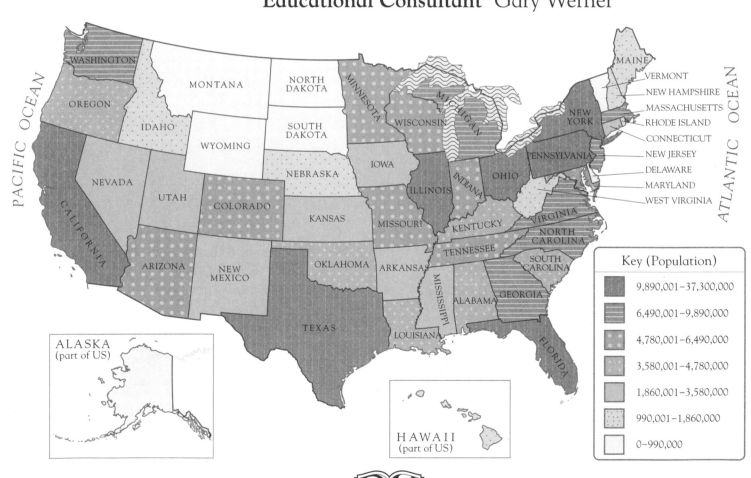

PACIFIC OCEAN

WASHINGTON
OREGON
IDAHO
MONTANA
NORTH DAKOTA
SOUTH DAKOTA
WYOMING
MINNESOTA
WISCONSIN
MICHIGAN
MAINE
VERMONT
NEW HAMPSHIRE
MASSACHUSETTS
RHODE ISLAND
CONNECTICUT
NEW JERSEY
DELAWARE
MARYLAND
WEST VIRGINIA
NEW YORK
PENNSYLVANIA
NEVADA
UTAH
COLORADO
NEBRASKA
IOWA
ILLINOIS
INDIANA
OHIO
CALIFORNIA
KANSAS
MISSOURI
KENTUCKY
VIRGINIA
NORTH CAROLINA
ARIZONA
NEW MEXICO
OKLAHOMA
ARKANSAS
TENNESSEE
SOUTH CAROLINA
MISSISSIPPI
ALABAMA
GEORGIA
TEXAS
LOUISIANA
FLORIDA

ATLANTIC OCEAN

ALASKA (part of US)

HAWAII (part of US)

Key (Population)

	9,890,001–37,300,000
	6,490,001–9,890,000
	4,780,001–6,490,000
	3,580,001–4,780,000
	1,860,001–3,580,000
	990,001–1,860,000
	0–990,000

DK

DK | Penguin Random House

US Editor Margaret Parrish
Editor Arpita Nath
Project Art Editor Tanvi Nathyal
Jacket Designer Dheeraj Arora
Cartography Team Deshpal Dabas,
Rajesh Mishra, Lokamata Sahu
Cartography Manager Suresh Kumar
Managing Editor Soma B. Chowdhury
Art Director Martin Wilson
DTP Designer Dheeraj Singh
Producer, Pre-Production Nadine King
Producer Priscilla Reby

First American Edition, 2016
Published in the United States by DK Publishing
1450 Broadway, Suite 801, New York, NY 10018

Copyright © 2016 Dorling Kindersley Limited
DK, a Divison of Penguin Random House LLC

20 10 9 8 7 6 5 4
004–285384–Jan/2016

A catalog record for this book
is available from the Library of Congress.
ISBN: 978-1-4654-4425-7

DK books are available at special discounts when purchased
in bulk for sales promotions, premiums, fund-raising, or
educational use. For details, contact: DK Publishing Special
Markets, 1450 Broadway, Suite 801, New York, NY 10018
SpecialSales@dk.com

Printed and bound in Canada

All images © Dorling Kindersley Limited
For further information see: www.dkimages.com

A WORLD OF IDEAS:
SEE ALL THERE IS TO KNOW
www.dk.com

Contents

This chart lists all the topics
in the book.

FACTS

Humans have always wanted to understand the world in which they live. Geography is one way to understand our world. Geography comes from the Greek words "Geo," which means "Earth," and "graphia," which means "writing." It is the study of Earth's physical features and how these features affect our lives. It tells us about the location and features of the places on Earth. Geography presents a picture of where we live. In a way, geography is a guidebook to life on Earth.

How well do you know your home planet, Earth? Read the statements below and check (✔) if each one is **true** or **false**. Read carefully, since some of these are tricky!

1. Most of the Earth's surface is covered in water.

   True ✓   False ☐

2. The Earth always rotates from west to east.

   True ✓   False ☐

3. North America is located below the equator.

   True ☐   False ✓

4. Globes show the Earth more accurately than flat maps.

   True ✓   False ☐

5. It takes the Earth 24 hours to revolve around the sun.

   True ☐   False ✓

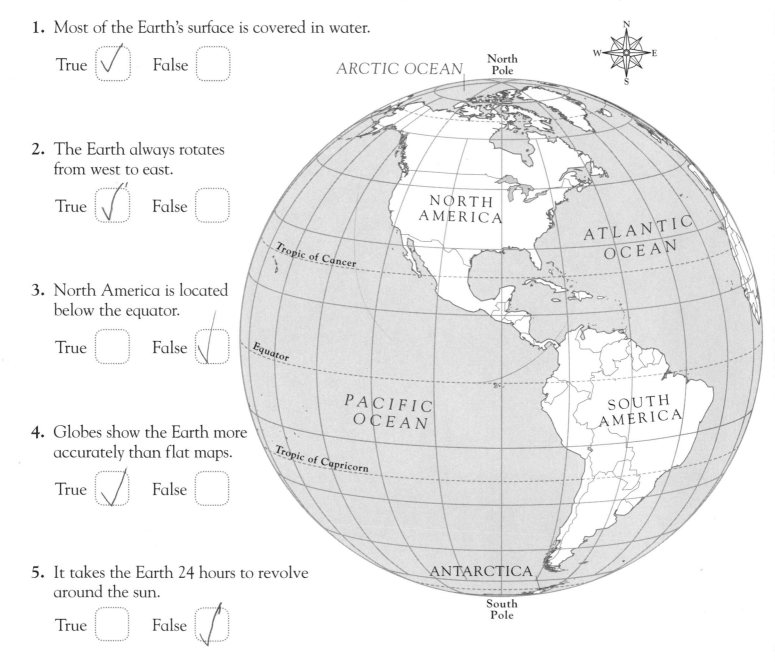

The surface of Earth is covered with many landforms and bodies of water—mountains and valleys, rain forests and deserts, rivers and oceans. Many of these natural features have been on our planet for millions of years. Over the past several thousand years, human beings have also built many important features on Earth to make life easier.

This map of part of the United States (US) shows some of its features—lakes, rivers, mountain peaks, cities, bridges, and highways. Look at the chart below. Put a check (✓) under **natural** or **built by humans** depending on the feature.

Feature	Natural	Built by Humans
Chicago, Illinois		✓
Great Salt Lake	✓	
Interstate Highway 40		✓
Gulf of Mexico	✓	
Kennedy Space Center		✓

★ Maps and Directions

FACTS

Maps are pictures that explain where places are in relation to each other. Maps help us to move from one place to another. They also describe how far one place is from another. Maps use directions to tell us where places are located. Mapmakers offer simple tools that help users make sense of maps.

Read the descriptions of the tools below and find them on this map of a city.

Compass Rose: Most maps have a tool called a compass rose. It shows the four directions—north, south, east, and west. The compass rose tells you which direction the top of the map is pointing toward.

Scale: Maps are pictures of very large places, and every map is smaller than the place it shows. The scale of a map tells you the distance an inch on a map represents, such as one mile or 1,000 miles.

Key or Legend: Maps use symbols to communicate information. These symbols, along with their explanations, are included in boxes on maps. These boxes are called keys or legends.

Key

✝ Church

🏛 Museum

ℹ Visitor center

✉ Post office

$ Bank

🎭 Theater

▒ Park

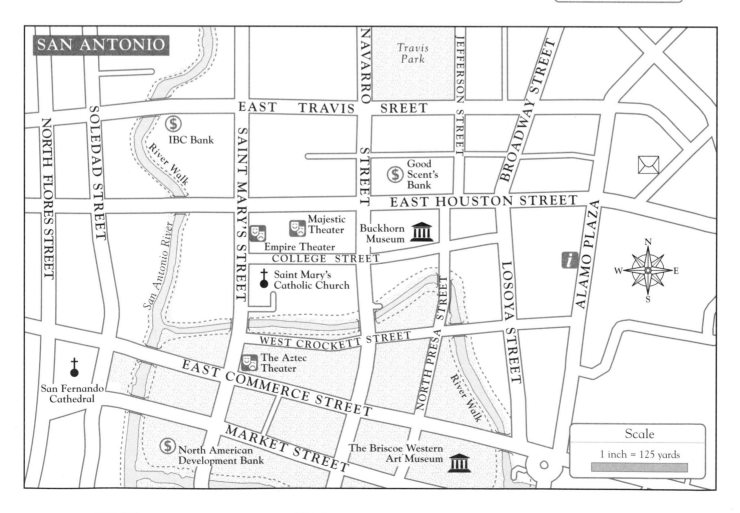

Flat maps do a good job of showing places on Earth. However, the best way to see things on the Earth is by putting a map on a rounded object—a globe. Flat maps have an advantage over globes: they are smaller and allow you to see everything at once. To see something on the other side of a globe, you must turn it. This may seem inconvenient, however, it is important because the Earth itself never stops spinning. Earth is tilted toward the sun and turns on an axis—an imaginary line that runs through the North Pole and South Pole. Flat maps do not spin, but globes do. This explains why a globe is the best way to represent Earth. It is shaped like our planet!

Take a look at the globe and the flat map pictured below. Fill in the chart by putting a check (✔) next to the one—**map** or **globe**—that shows the feature better.

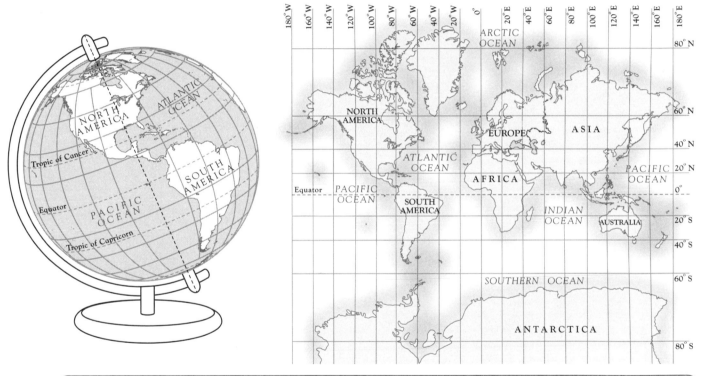

Feature	Map	Globe
Easier to carry		
Shows a more accurate picture of what Earth looks like		
Shows all places at a glance		
Models how Earth spins on its axis		
More convenient for adding extra information		

FACTS

Globes are the best way to represent the spherical shape of the Earth, but flat maps are more convenient. The representation of a round Earth on a flat map is called a projection. While making projections, mapmakers have to distort the shape and size of the land in some ways. There are many types of projections. Here are two of them:

Mercator projection: This projection is good for showing directions, but distances and size of lands away from the equator are distorted.

Interrupted projection: Shapes and sizes of land are accurate on this projection, but distance and directions are distorted.

Look at the Mercator and Interrupted map projections and then answer the questions.

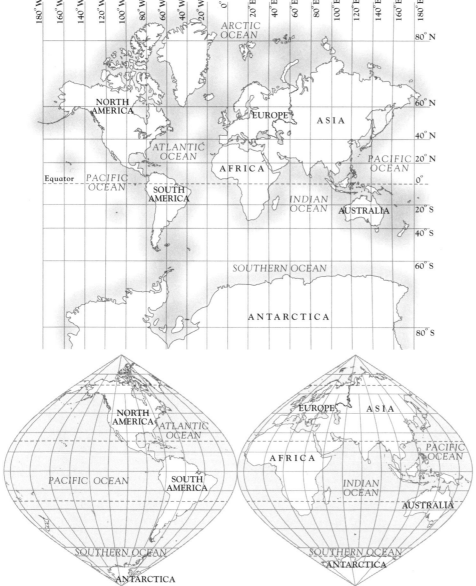

Mercator projection

Interrupted projection

1. Which map projection would be easier to use for planning a trip?

....

2. On which map projection does Africa look larger? Which is more accurate?

....
....
....
....
....
....

3. On which map projection can you see Europe clearly?

....

4. Which map projection do you prefer and why?

....
....
....
....

We can divide the Earth into halves by using two imaginary lines. Each half is called a hemisphere, meaning "half of a round object." The equator is the imaginary line around the middle of the Earth that divides it into the northern hemisphere and the southern hemisphere. The prime meridian is the imaginary line running vertically from the North Pole to the South Pole. The area east of the prime meridian is the eastern hemisphere and the area west of it is the western hemisphere.

The maps show the four hemispheres. Look at the maps and then check (✔) the hemispheres in which the continents appear. **Note:** Some continents may fall in all four hemispheres.

Northern hemisphere (N)

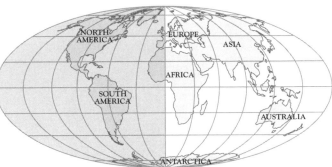

Western hemisphere (W)

Southern hemisphere (S)

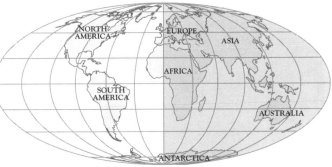

Eastern hemisphere (E)

Continents	Northern (N)	Southern (S)	Western (W)	Eastern (E)
Africa	✔			✔
Antarctica		✔		✔
Asia	✔			✔
Australia		✔		✔
Europe	✔			✔
North America	✔		✔	
South America	✔	✔	✔	

★ Oceans

More than two-thirds of Earth's surface is covered by water. The five oceans are the biggest bodies of water on Earth. The Pacific Ocean is the largest ocean, followed by the Atlantic, the Indian, the Southern, and the Arctic oceans. The Pacific is so large that you could fit all of Earth's land inside it! The saltwater oceans contain about 96 percent of all the water on Earth. All other bodies of water, such as rivers, lakes, and ponds, make up only four percent.

Study this map showing the oceans on Earth. Then answer the questions below.

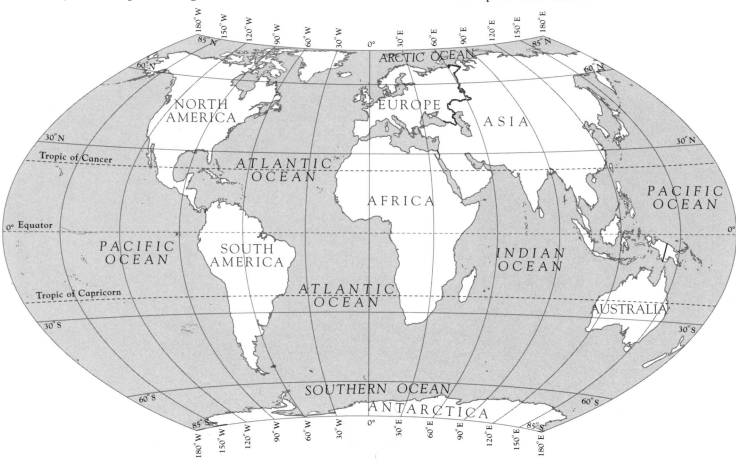

1. If you sail west from the southern tip of Africa, on which ocean would you be?

   ATLantic ocean

2. Which ocean is located between east Africa and Australia?

   Indail ocean

3. Which ocean surrounds the North Pole?

   arctic ocean

4. Which three oceans on the Earth does the equator cross?

   Indain ocean, Pacific, Atlantic

5. If you stand at the southern tip of South America, which ocean would lie south of you?

   Southern ocean

FACTS

The Earth is divided into seven large masses of land known as continents. Asia is the largest of the seven continents, followed by Africa, North America, South America, Antarctica, Europe, and Australia. Scientists estimate that two-thirds of all land is in the northern hemisphere and one-third is in the southern hemisphere. Scientists believe that the continents were once a big, connected landmass called Pangaea. This supercontinent was located in the middle of a super ocean.

Study this map of Earth's seven continents. Then answer the questions below.

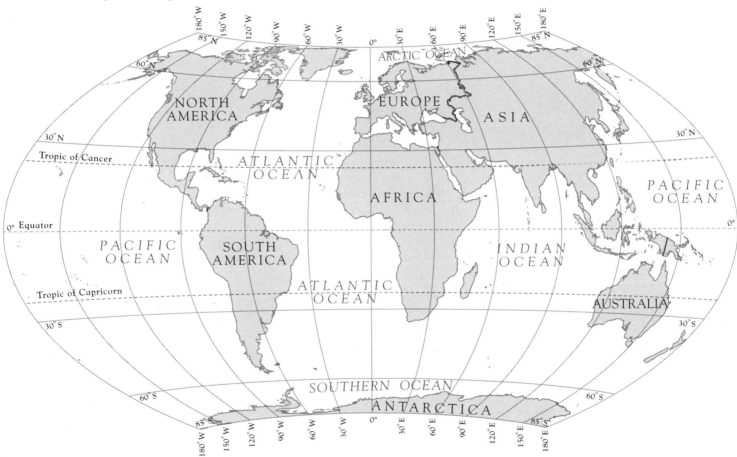

1. This continent has borders on the Atlantic and Pacific oceans, and is located north of the equator.

....

2. Divided almost in half by the equator, this continent is west of the Indian Ocean.

....

3. This is the largest continent on Earth, with borders on the Arctic, Pacific, and Indian oceans.

....

4. This small continent is west of Asia and east of North America.

....

The Earth is huge, so it can be difficult to give a precise location for any place on the planet. To address that problem, a grid with imaginary crisscrossing lines is used on globes and maps. The places where the lines meet are assigned numbers, providing an exact location. The imaginary, parallel, horizontal lines that run from east to west are known as latitudes. They are measured in degrees north and south. The imaginary horizontal line found at 0°, midway between the North Pole and the South Pole, is known as the equator. All other latitude lines are north or south of the equator. So, the North Pole is 90° north of the equator and the South Pole is 90° south. Lines in between are at 1° to 89° north or south.

Look at this map of some US cities. Use the latitudes to answer the questions.

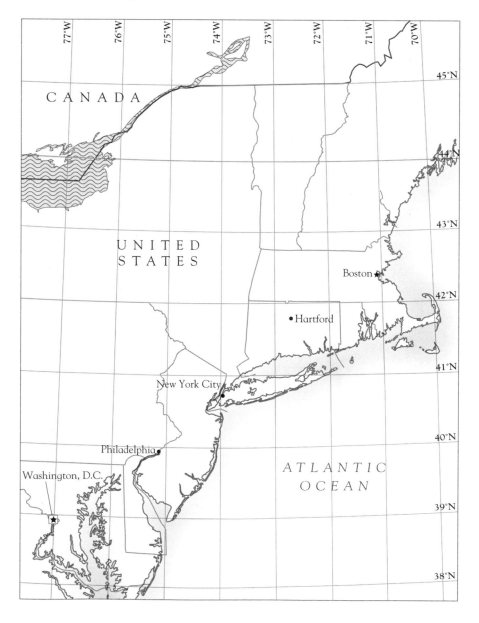

1. Which city lies between 42°N and 43°N?

   ....

2. Which city lies between 41°N and 42°N?

   ....

3. Which city lies between 40°N and 41°N?

   ....

4. Which city lies between 39°N and 40°N?

   ....

5. Which city lies between 38°N and 39°N?

   ....

Key	
★	Country capital
⋆	State capital
•	Major city
〰	Lake

Longitudes are imaginary lines that run from north to south across the Earth, meeting at the North Pole and South Pole. The 0° line is the prime meridian. Longitudes are measured in degrees east and west.

This map shows North America with its longitudes and latitudes. Look at the map and answer the questions.

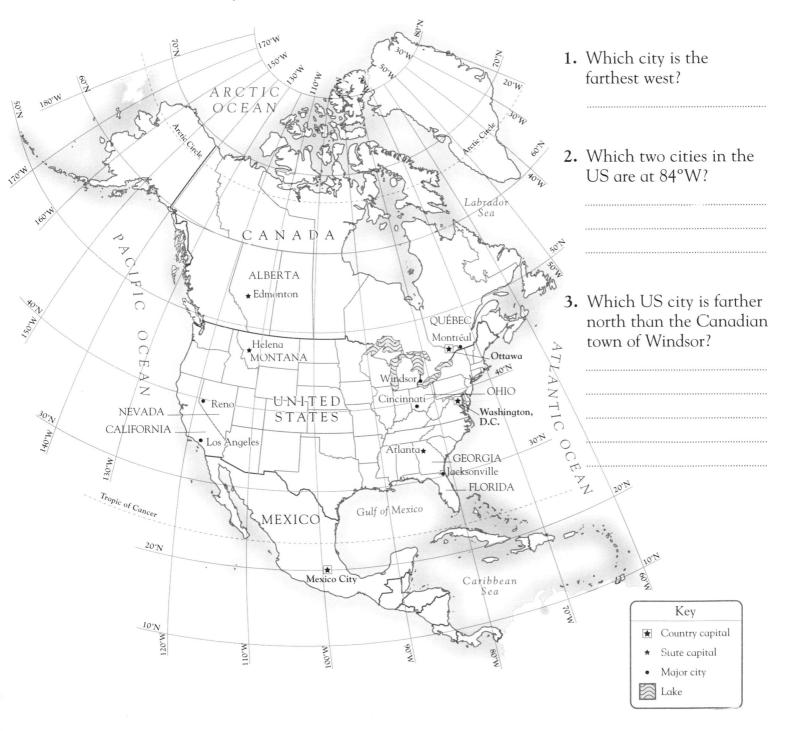

1. Which city is the farthest west?

....

2. Which two cities in the US are at 84°W?

....

....

....

3. Which US city is farther north than the Canadian town of Windsor?

....

....

....

....

Key

★ Country capital

★ State capital

• Major city

〰 Lake

FACTS

The Earth is always spinning on its axis. As the Earth turns, one-half points toward the sun (daytime) and the other half points away (nighttime). It takes the Earth 24 hours to complete one spin. To calculate the time in other parts of the world, time zones were created. Time zones are 24 vertical slices of the Earth.

On this time-zone map, it is 12 PM in London, England; Lisbon, Portugal; and Casablanca, Morocco. In the next zone to the east—which includes Paris, France, and Lagos, Nigeria—it is 1 PM. If you look at the United States, you will see that it is 7 AM in Washington, D.C., as well as in Lima, Peru. Look at the map carefully and figure out the time in places around the world.

1. When it is noon (12:00 PM) in London, what time is it in Sydney, Australia?

   ....

2. China has its own single time zone. When it is 8 PM in Beijing, China, what time is it in Honolulu, Hawaii?

   ....

3. When it is noon in Moscow, Russia, what time is it in Saudi Arabia and Kenya?

   ....

4. When it is midnight (12:00 AM) in London, what time is it in New York City?

   ....

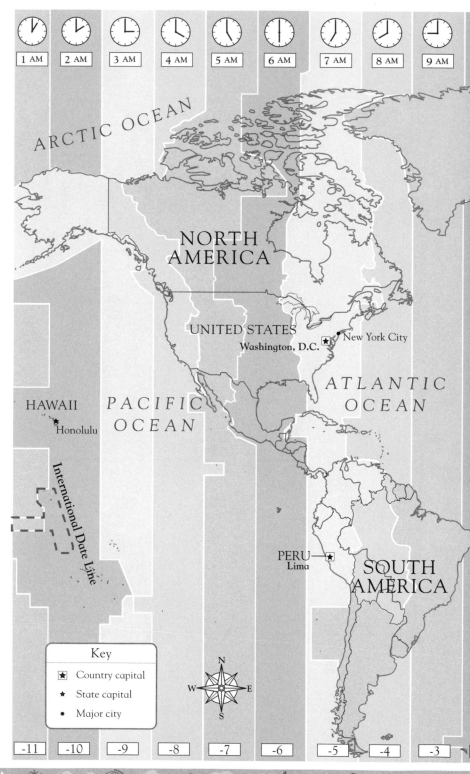

These imaginary slices run from the North Pole to the South Pole. Each time zone represents one hour. Since the Earth rotates from west to east, the time in every zone is one hour later than the next zone to the west. A few large countries—including India and China—have created their own time zones.

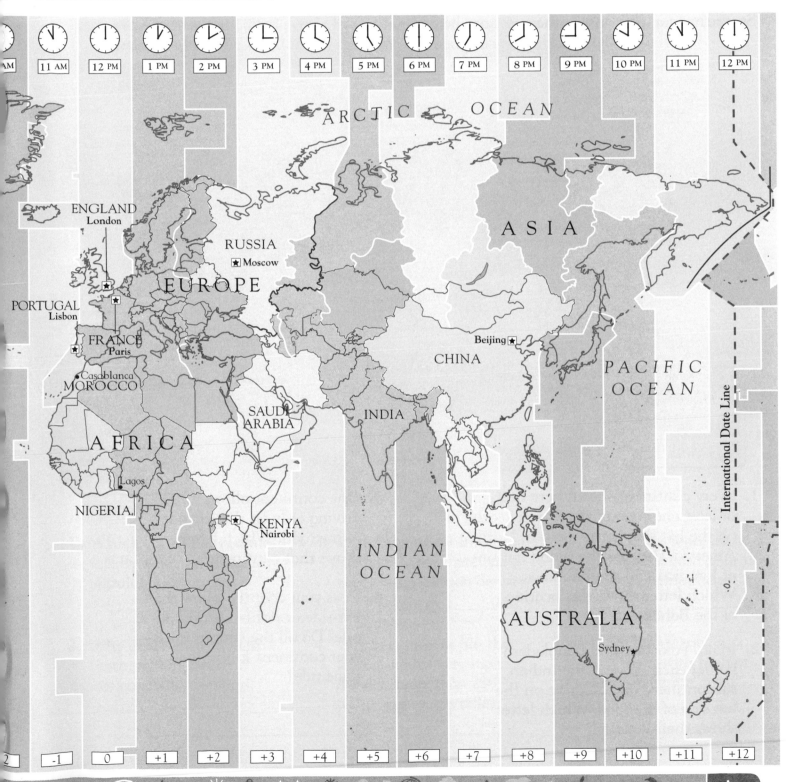

FACTS

Earth is covered with physical features, such as mountains, plains, plateaus, deserts, rivers, lakes, and forests. The physical features of a place affect the ways people use the land. For example, some flatlands with rich soil could be suitable for growing crops, whereas other flatlands are better for raising livestock.

The United States has many major physical features. This map shows some of those features. Use the map to identify the features mentioned in the descriptions below.

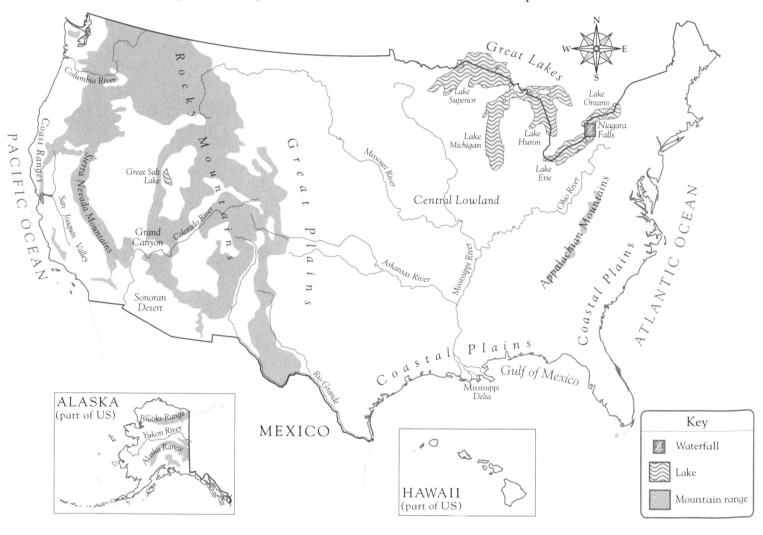

1. This is an agriculturally important valley that lies between the Sierra Nevada Mountains and the Coast Ranges.

   ....

2. This is the longest mountain range in the US.

   ....

3. This is a river that forms part of the US border with Mexico.

   ....

4. This is a chain of five large neighboring lakes.

   ....

Physical Features: Mountains

Mountains are landforms that rise from the Earth to a height far above the surrounding land. While some mountains are very steep, others slope up gradually. Mountains are found on all the seven continents. A few stand alone, but many are part of mountain ranges.

"The Seven Summits" is the name given to the highest mountain peaks on the seven continents. Read the descriptions of the peaks below. On the map, write the number that matches their location.

1. The world's highest peak, Mount Everest, is located in Asia. It is 29,029 ft high.

2. Located in the Andes in South America, Mount Aconcagua is 22,831 ft tall.

3. Denali, also called Mount McKinley, is North America's highest peak, at 20,310 ft.

4. Mount Kilimanjaro is the highest peak in Africa, at 19,341 ft.

5. Mount Elbrus of the Caucasus range in Europe is 18,510 ft high.

6. Antarctica's highest peak is the Vinson Massif. It is 16,050 ft high.

7. Mount Kosciuszko is Australia's highest peak, at 7,310 ft.

FACTS

Rivers are large flowing bodies of water found all over the world. They are usually, though not always, freshwater. Rivers were very important to early humans, providing food, drinking water, a place to wash, and a way to travel long distances. Rivers remain vital to life on Earth today. Some rivers are enormous. For example, the Amazon River in South America and the Nile River in Africa are both more than 4,000 miles long.

This map shows the 10 longest rivers that flow through the United States. Locate them on the map and find the names in the wordsearch below.

C	O	L	O	R	A	D	O	H	V	K	M	D	N	O	X	L	J	P
Y	Y	R	H	D	Q	M	I	S	S	I	S	S	I	P	P	I	L	O
U	C	E	L	X	A	R	K	A	N	S	A	S	C	L	T	D	Y	H
K	Q	D	F	C	O	L	U	M	B	I	A	G	A	V	R	O	J	I
O	X	C	L	T	V	J	M	I	S	S	O	U	R	I	U	L	B	O
N	S	N	A	K	E	Y	B	N	P	R	I	O	G	R	A	N	D	E

FACTS

Deserts are areas where water is scarce and where it rarely rains. A desert need not be hot and sandy. If a place receives less than 10 inches of rain or snowfall in a year, it is considered a desert. Frozen Antarctica is a desert, for example. Probably the world's most famous desert is the Sahara, a huge sandy stretch across North Africa. Deserts are among the most difficult places to live. A small number of plants and animals thrive there, such as cacti, lizards, and camels.

This map shows the major deserts on Earth (excluding the polar regions). Use the map to answer the questions below.

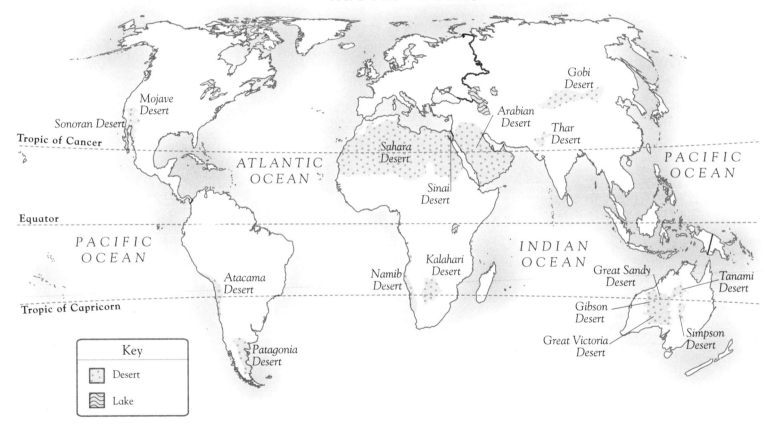

1. Label the continents shown. Which continent does not have a major desert?

....

2. This continent has five deserts, which are located very close to one another.

....

3. In which region of North America are most deserts located?

....

4. What is the name of the large desert in Central Asia?

....

FACTS

Rain forests are wet areas with dense vegetation. They cover only two percent of the Earth's surface, but half of all animal and plant species are found in them. The three largest rain forests are the Amazon in South America, the Congo Basin in Africa, and the Southeast Asian rain forest. Rain forests are extremely important to life on Earth, but humans are tearing down parts of them. Scientists warn that we need to preserve rain forests and protect the creatures living in them to keep our planet healthy.

Most rain forests are divided vertically into four very different layers. They are **forest floor**, **understory**, **canopy**, and **emergent**. Look at this picture of a rain forest below. Read the descriptions and identify each layer. First, write the name of the layer on the picture. Then write the number of the layer next to its correct description.

Description
It is pretty dark here. Plants have large leaves to catch as much of the little light that peeks through. The red-eyed tree frog lives under the many plants here.
Eagles, bats, and butterflies love it up here. The sun's rays are strong and the tallest trees emerge above the forest. Skilled climbing animals can clamber around in the sun.
This is the coolest, darkest, and dampest layer. Among the trunks of tall trees, animals crawl in the soil. Giant anteaters search the ground for food here.
Here there is an excellent mix of sunshine and shadow. The leaves of the tallest trees offer lots of shade here. Sunshine warms up the place but it is not too hot for toucans and some other birds. There is a maze of branches and tree trunks for frisky monkeys to jump from one tree to another.

1.

2.

3.

4.

Physical Features: Biomes

A biome is an area with distinct vegetation, climate, and animal life. Types of biomes include forests, deserts, grasslands, and tundra. Biomes can be further divided. For example, all deserts get little rain, but there are hot deserts, such as the Sahara; warm, semiarid deserts, such as the Great Basin Desert in the US; cool, coastal deserts, such as the Atacama in Chile; and cold polar deserts, such as Antarctica. Animals that thrive in one biome are unlikely to survive in others.

There are three major types of forest biome. Read the chart and answer the questions below.

Name of Biome	Description	Where Found	Animals Found
Tropical (Rain forest)	Warm and rainy all year. Little light filters down to the floor of these dense, dark forests. This biome is greatly endangered.	In warm climates, often near the equator, in North America, South America, Africa, Australia, and Asia	Tropical birds, bats, insects, and small mammals
Temperate (Deciduous)	Warm in summer, cold in winter, and rainy all year. In summer, broadleaf trees let some sunlight reach the forest floor. In colder months, leaves fall off trees.	Moderate climate areas of North and South America, northeastern Asia, and Western and Central Europe	Squirrels, deer, rabbits, skunks, bears, wolves, mountain lions, bald eagles, and bobcats
Boreal (Taiga)	Evergreen forests with short, wet, warm summers and long, dry, cold winters. Thick, dense trees with needles instead of leaves prevent much light from reaching the forest floor.	Cold northern areas of Eurasia and North America, including Siberia, Alaska, northern Canada, and Scandinavian countries	Moose, bears, weasels, foxes, wolves, deer, bald eagles, and hawks

1. Which type of forest goes through the most dramatic change in appearance over the course of a year? How does it change?

   ....

   ....

2. One of these biomes is not found in the southern hemisphere. Which one is it?

   ....

3. Which continent is not listed on this chart?

   ....

   ....

4. Which biome has the least amount of rainfall?

   ....

5. In which biome will you find moose?

FACTS

North America is Earth's third-largest continent. It is located in the northern and western hemispheres and has everything from glaciers to rain forests. North America's climate changes radically from north to south. Alaska, parts of northern Canada, and Greenland have very cold winters. The middle regions are mostly temperate and the southern regions are tropical.

Study this map of North America showing some of its physical features. Find the letter on the map that matches the descriptions given below, then write the letter next to the description.

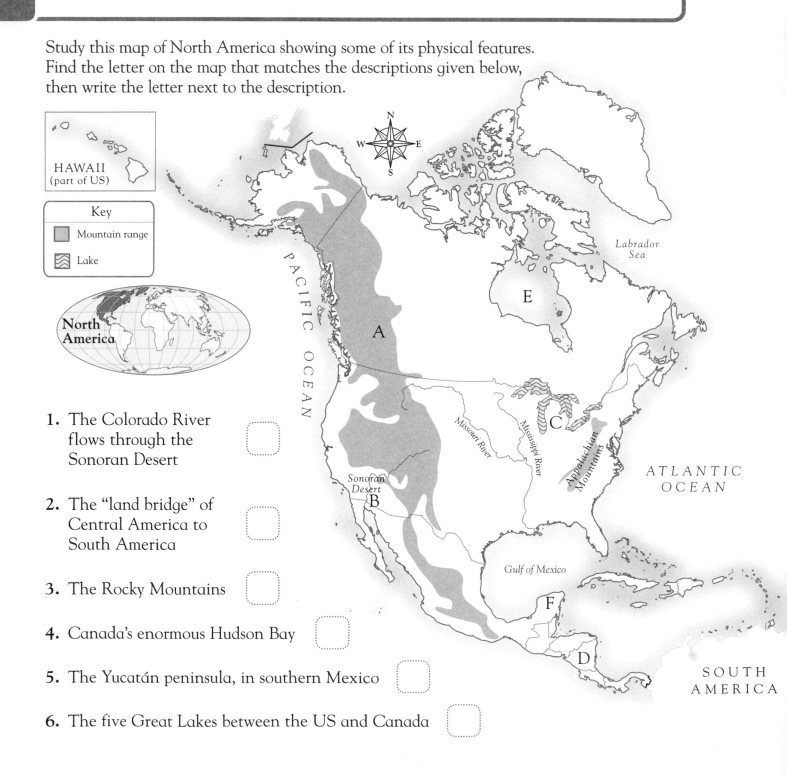

HAWAII (part of US)

Key
- Mountain range
- Lake

North America

1. The Colorado River flows through the Sonoran Desert

2. The "land bridge" of Central America to South America

3. The Rocky Mountains

4. Canada's enormous Hudson Bay

5. The Yucatán peninsula, in southern Mexico

6. The five Great Lakes between the US and Canada

North America is made up of three very large countries—the United States, Canada, and Mexico. The continent also includes the smaller countries of Central America, such as Panama, Guatemala, and Costa Rica, and the island nations of the Caribbean, such as Dominican Republic, Cuba, Jamaica, and Haiti. Greenland, the world's largest island, is also a part of North America. However, it is a territory of the European country of Denmark.

Study this political map of North America. Then read the descriptions given below. On the map, write the letter that matches each description.

A. This large island nation is located just 90 miles south of Florida.

B. This country shares two separate borders with the US.

C. This large island is made up of two countries.

D. This country has coasts on the Atlantic Ocean, the Pacific Ocean, and the Gulf of Mexico.

E. This southernmost nation has a canal linking the Atlantic and Pacific oceans.

GREENLAND
(to Denmark)

ALASKA
(part of US)

PACIFIC OCEAN

CANADA

UNITED STATES
OF AMERICA

ATLANTIC OCEAN

MEXICO

Gulf of Mexico

THE BAHAMAS

PUERTO RICO (part of US)

DOMINICAN
REPUBLIC

ANTIGUA & BARBUDA

DOMINICA

CUBA

ST. KITTS
& NEVIS

ST. LUCIA

HAITI

BARBADOS

JAMAICA

GRENADA

ST. VINCENT &
THE GRENADINES

BELIZE

HONDURAS

Caribbean Sea

TRINIDAD & TOBAGO

GUATEMALA
EL SALVADOR
NICARAGUA
COSTA RICA
PANAMA

SOUTH
AMERICA

HAWAII
(part of US)

United States: States and Population

The United States of America, stretching from the Atlantic Ocean to the Pacific Ocean, is home to more than 300 million people. It has 50 states, 48 of which are contiguous (connected). The other two states are Alaska, bordering Canada in the far north, and Hawaii, a series of islands in the Pacific Ocean.

The total population of the United States, according to the 2010 Census, was 308,745,538. This map is based on the 2010 Census and shows the differences in population across the 50 states. Use the map to answer the questions below.

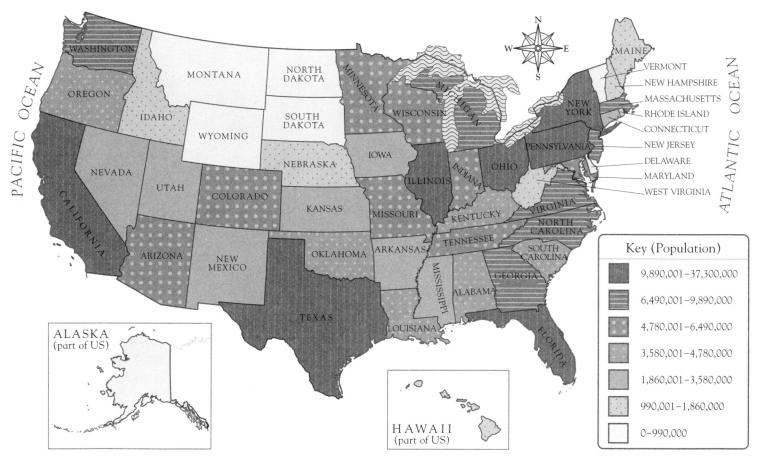

1. Name the seven most populous states with a population of 9,890,001 or more.

....

....

....

2. Which combination of states has a greater population—North and South Dakota or North and South Carolina?

....

3. Alaska is one of the states with a population of 990,000 or less. Name the other six.

....

....

....

4. Of the three states on the west coast, which has the largest population?

....

United States: Capital Cities

FACTS

Capital cities are places where the branches of government are located. The capital of the United States is Washington, D.C., but each of the 50 states also has a capital. Sometimes, the capital is the largest city in the state—for example, Atlanta, Georgia. However, for most states in the US, the capital is a less populous city. For example, the capital of New York State is not New York City, with its eight million residents, but Albany, with a population below 150,000.

This map shows the capital cities of the 48 contiguous states in the US.
Use the map to answer the questions below.

Key
- ⊡ Country capital
- ★ State capital
- ▨ Lake

1. Four state capitals have the word "city" in their names. One is Oklahoma City. Name the other three.

   ....

   ....

2. The capital cities of two states are named after the explorer who arrived in the New World in 1492. Name the states and their capitals.

   ....

   ....

3. Jefferson City is one of four state capital cities named after a former US president. Below are the other three capital cities. Write the name of each state.

   Madison ....

   Jackson ....

   Lincoln ....

4. Which two state capitals are located on the Mississippi River?

United States: Alaska and Hawaii

Alaska and Hawaii became the 49th and 50th states of the US, respectively, in 1959. They are the only two US states separated by land or water from the other 48. Located near the Arctic Circle, Alaska is the largest US state and has a cold climate most of the year. Hawaii is a series of small islands in the Pacific Ocean and has a warm climate all year.

Study these maps of Alaska and Hawaii. Then answer the questions below.

1. Study the longitudes in both maps. Which of the two states—Alaska or Hawaii—extends more to the west?

   ....

2. Name the capital cities of Alaska and Hawaii.

   ....

   ....

3. Using what you have read above about Alaska and Hawaii, which state do you think would be more likely to grow pineapples and coconuts? Why do you think so?

   ....

   ....

   ....

FACTS

The United States is a large country, and it crosses six time zones. In the 48 contiguous states, there are four time zones. Therefore, when it is 9 AM in the Eastern Time Zone, it will be 8 AM in the Central Time Zone, 7 AM in the Mountain Time Zone, and 6 AM in the Pacific Time Zone. As for the other two states, it will be 5 AM in Alaska, which is in the Alaskan Time Zone, and, in standard time, 4 AM in Hawaii, which is located in the Hawaii-Aleutian Time Zone.

Study this map of the US showing the different time zones. For each city, a time has been given. Write what the time will be in Denver, Colorado.
Note: Use the map on p.14 to help you.

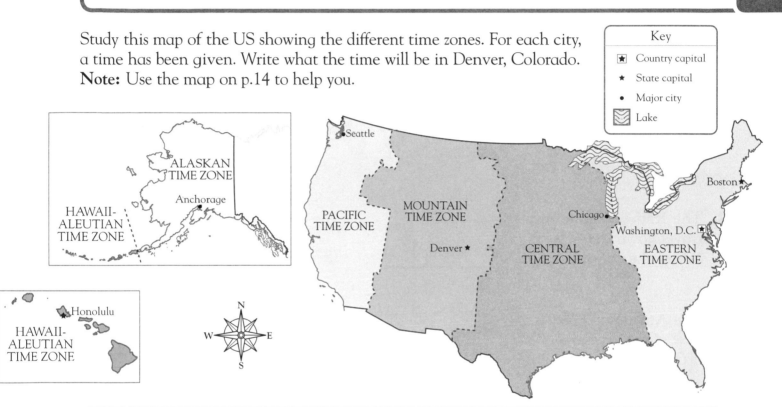

Cities and Their Times	Time in Denver, CO
Honolulu, HI, 10 AM	
Seattle, WA, 11 AM	
Boston, MA 1 PM	
Chicago, IL, 4 PM	
Anchorage, AK, 12 PM	

If you were phoning from Denver, list the five cities in the order you will need to make the calls.

....

....

Europe: Physical Features

FACTS

Europe, Earth's second-smallest continent, is located in the northern, eastern, and western hemispheres. It is attached to Asia, and together they make up one big supercontinent called Eurasia. Europe has many peninsulas—land connected to the mainland but surrounded by water on three sides. It is surrounded by the Arctic and Atlantic oceans in the north and west, and by the Mediterranean and Black seas in the south. It has some major mountain ranges, such as the Alps, Pyrenees, and Urals.

Study this map of Europe showing some of its physical features. Then complete the sentences.

1. .... Mountains run down the center of Italy.

2. The Kola Peninsula juts out into the .... Sea.

3. The .... separates Europe from Africa.

4. The Tagus River flows through Spain and Portugal before emptying into the .... Ocean.

Key
- - - - Disputed boundary

≋ Lake

▨ Mountain range

Barents Sea

Kola Peninsula

Ural Mountains

ASIA

Norwegian Sea

Europe

Lake Onega

Gulf of Bothnia

Lake Vanern

Lake Ladoga

ATLANTIC OCEAN

North Sea

Lake Vattern

Baltic Sea

Western Dvina River

Volga River

North European Plain

N W E S

Thames River

Elbe River

Weser River

Oder River

Vistula River

Dnieper River

English Channel

Rhine River

Seine River

Danube River

Don River

Loire River

Carpathian Mountains

Sea of Azov

Bay of Biscay

Alps

Caucasus Mountains

Caspian Sea

PORTUGAL

Po River

Balkan Mountains

Black Sea

SPAIN

Pyrenees

Apennine Mountains

ITALY

Adriatic Sea

ASIA

Tagus River

Iberian Peninsula

Strait of Gibraltar

Mediterranean Sea

Tyrrhenian Sea

Ionian Sea

AFRICA

About 750 million people live in Europe, making it Earth's third-most populous continent. Russia, Germany, France, the United Kingdom, and Italy are the most populated countries of Europe. Today, most of its countries are connected in an economic and political entity known as the European Union.

Unscramble the names of the countries given below. Then, using this political map of Europe, find and write the capitals of these countries.

Scrambled Words	Country Name	Capital City
Nesdew		
Namrgey		
Yhgurna		
Danrile		

Europe

Key
- - - Disputed boundary
★ Country capital

ICELAND
Reykjavík

Norwegian Sea

Barents Sea

Ural Mountains

ASIA

ATLANTIC OCEAN

IRELAND
Dublin

NORWAY
Oslo

FINLAND
Helsinki

SWEDEN
Stockholm

ESTONIA
Tallinn

LATVIA
Riga

RUSSIA
Moscow

DENMARK
Copenhagen

NETHERLANDS
Amsterdam

KALININGRAD
(Russia)

LITHUANIA
Vilnius

ENGLAND
London

BELGIUM
Brussels

GERMANY
Berlin

POLAND
Warsaw

BELARUS
Minsk

LUXEMBOURG
Luxembourg

FRANCE
Paris

CZECH REPUBLIC
Prague

SLOVAKIA
Bratislava

UKRAINE
Kiev

LIECHTENSTEIN
Vaduz

SWITZERLAND
Bern

AUSTRIA
Vienna

HUNGARY
Budapest

MOLDOVA
Chişinău

PORTUGAL
Lisbon

ANDORRA
Andorra la Vella

MONACO
Monaco

SLOVENIA
Ljubljana

CROATIA
Zagreb

SERBIA
Belgrade

ROMANIA
Bucharest

Black Sea

Caspian Sea

SPAIN
Madrid

SAN MARINO
San Marino

VATICAN CITY

KOSOVO
Priština

BOSNIA-HERZEGOVINA
Sarajevo

ITALY
Rome

BULGARIA
Sofia

TURKEY

MONTENEGRO
Podgorica

MACEDONIA
Skopje

Mediterranean Sea

ASIA

AFRICA

MALTA
Valletta

ALBANIA
Tirana

Greece
Athens

FACTS

Asia is the largest continent on Earth. It is located in the northern and eastern hemispheres. Although it is on the same landmass as Europe, Asia is separated from Europe by the Ural Mountains and the Caspian Sea. This continent is home to the world's tallest mountain chain—the Himalayas; Earth's lowest point—the Dead Sea; and Earth's highest plateau—the Tibetan Plateau. It has a large desert, the Gobi, and vast rivers—Ganges in India, Huang He in China, and Mekong in Vietnam. More than 4.3 billion people reside in Asia. This is more than half of the world's population. The world's most populous countries, China and India, are located in Asia.

Study this map of Asia showing its physical features and political divisions. Then fill in the answers in the crossword puzzle on the following page.

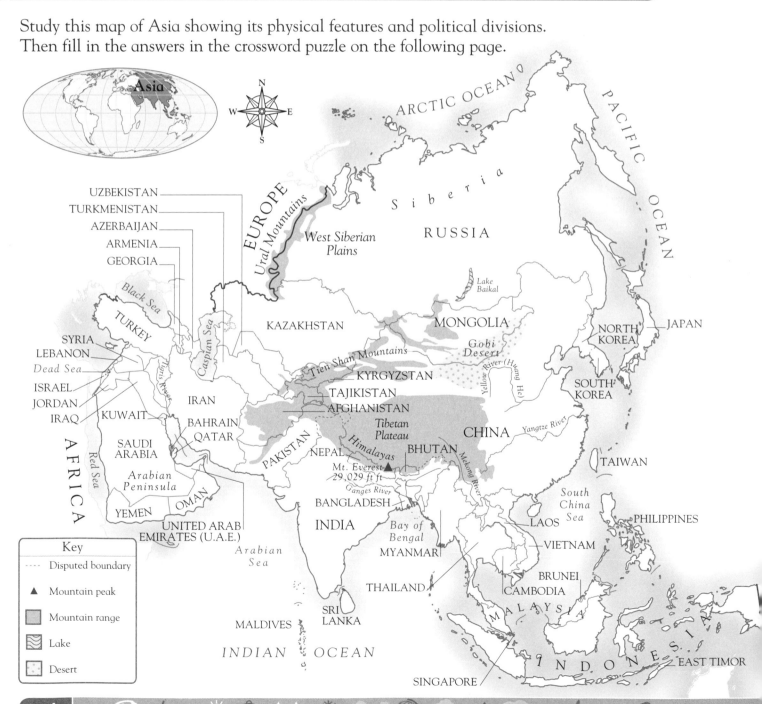

Read the descriptions of some of Asia's important physical features and political divisions. Then, using the map on the previous page, complete the crossword.

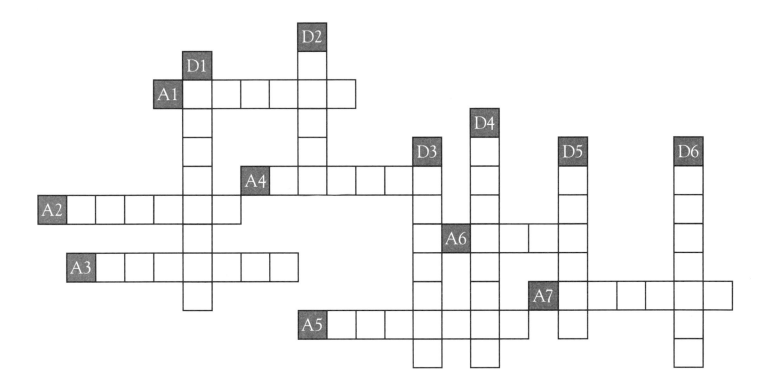

Across
1. A river that forms part of the border between Laos and Thailand
2. A major river that flows through Iraq
3. The Earth's highest and biggest plateau, located in Central Asia
4. A major river that flows through India
5. An ocean surrounding Asia on the east
6. A large desert that stretches across Mongolia and China
7. An ocean north of Russia

Down
1. A cluster of small islands in the Indian Ocean, southwest of Sri Lanka
2. Earth's second most populous nation, located south of the Himalayas
3. The northernmost region of Asia, which has a very cold climate
4. A landlocked country between Russia in the north and China in the south
5. An island country located some miles off the southeast coast of China
6. A landlocked lake, called a "sea," forming part of Kazakhstan's border

⭐ Africa: Physical Features

FACTS

Africa is the second-largest continent on Earth. It extends over the four hemispheres. It is bordered by the Mediterranean Sea in the north, the Red Sea and the Indian Ocean in the east, and the Atlantic Ocean in the west. Africa is home to the world's largest desert—the Sahara; the world's longest river—the Nile; one of the world's biggest waterfalls—Victoria Falls; and the world's second-largest rain forest—Congo Basin. Africa's remarkable wildlife includes camels, gorillas, giraffes, elephants, and lions.

Read the descriptions of some of Africa's physical features below. On the map, write the number at the location that matches each description.

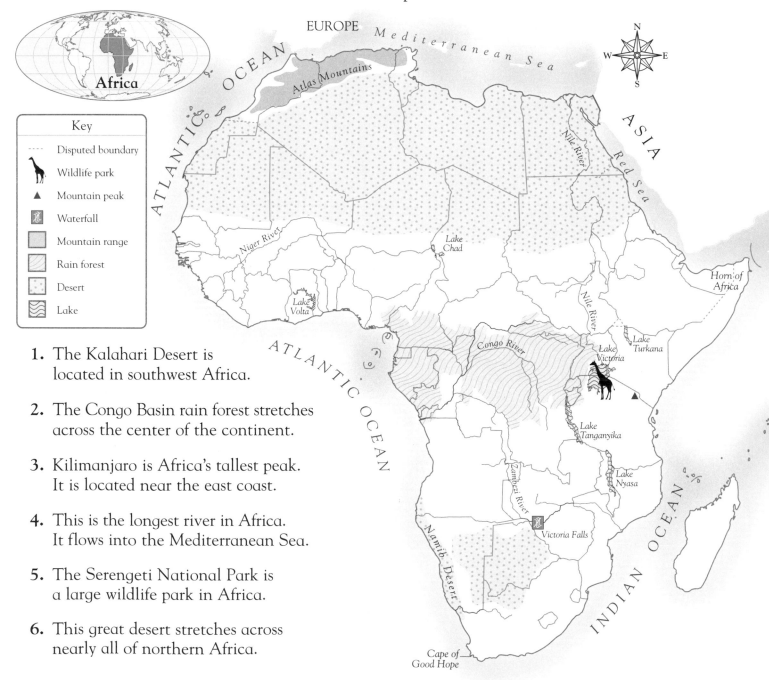

Key
- ┈┈┈ Disputed boundary
- 🦒 Wildlife park
- ▲ Mountain peak
- 🏞 Waterfall
- ▨ Mountain range
- ▨ Rain forest
- ⦂⦂ Desert
- 〰 Lake

1. The Kalahari Desert is located in southwest Africa.

2. The Congo Basin rain forest stretches across the center of the continent.

3. Kilimanjaro is Africa's tallest peak. It is located near the east coast.

4. This is the longest river in Africa. It flows into the Mediterranean Sea.

5. The Serengeti National Park is a large wildlife park in Africa.

6. This great desert stretches across nearly all of northern Africa.

FACTS

Africa is Earth's second most populous continent, after Asia. It is home to over a billion people who live in its 54 nations. Nigeria, Africa's most populated country, has more than 170 million residents. Egypt, Ethiopia, South Africa, and Congo also have large populations. About 100 years ago, almost all of Africa was colonized by European countries. Today, however, Africa is made up of independent nations. It has vast reserves of natural resources, such as oil, natural gas, and minerals.

This political map of Africa shows its valuable natural resources. Use the map to answer the questions below.

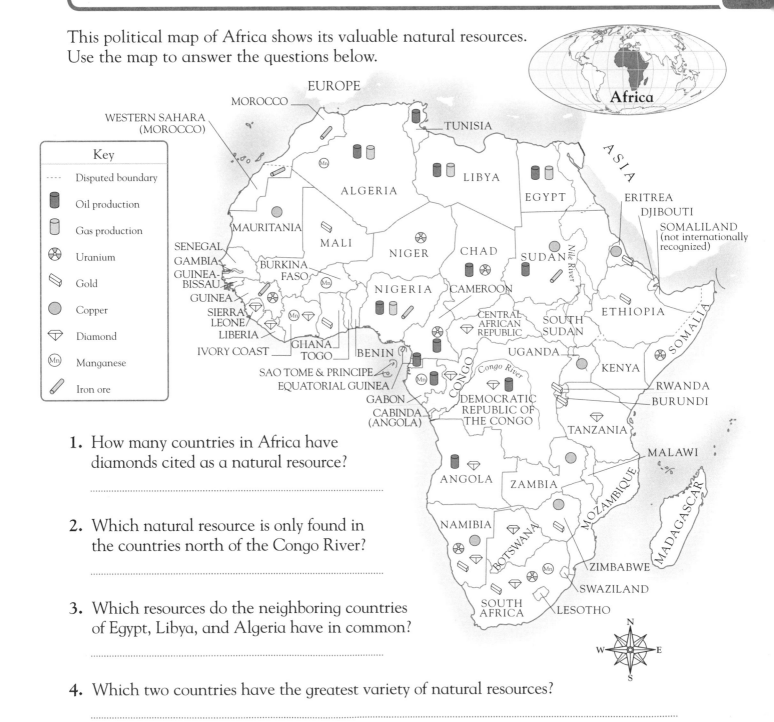

Key

- - - - Disputed boundary
- Oil production
- Gas production
- ⊛ Uranium
- Gold
- Copper
- ▽ Diamond
- (Mn) Manganese
- Iron ore

1. How many countries in Africa have diamonds cited as a natural resource?

2. Which natural resource is only found in the countries north of the Congo River?

3. Which resources do the neighboring countries of Egypt, Libya, and Algeria have in common?

4. Which two countries have the greatest variety of natural resources?

Australia is the smallest of all continents on Earth. It is nicknamed "the land down under" because it is the only inhabited continent that does not extend above the equator. Australia is also the only continent made up of just one country, and the only one that is an island, not touching any other landmass. Australia is bordered by the Indian Ocean on the west and the Pacific Ocean on the east.

Look at this map showing Australia's provinces and natural features. Read the descriptions below and write the name of the location.

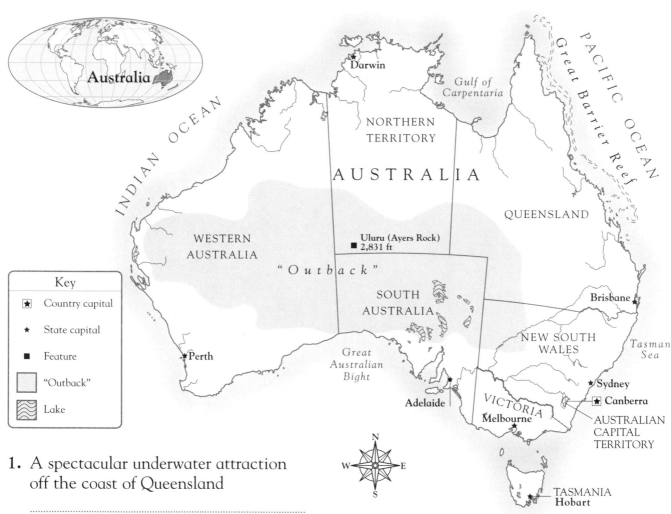

1. A spectacular underwater attraction off the coast of Queensland

   ....

2. The Australian State that is a separate island

   ....

4. A major city on the west coast of Australia

   ....

3. Australia's northernmost city, named after a scientist

   ....

5. A huge sandstone rock located in the Northern Territory

   ....

Antarctica is the frozen continent surrounding the South Pole. It is the fifth-largest continent (bigger only than Europe and Australia). About 98 percent of Antarctica is covered with a thick sheet of ice all year. It gets very, very cold there. In July 1983, the temperature at Vostok Research Station went down to −128.6 °F (−89.2 °C). It was the lowest temperature ever recorded on Earth. The only people living on Antarctica are involved in scientific study.

Here are some facts about Antarctica. Cross out the wrong word from the two options given to make the fact correct.

Antarctica

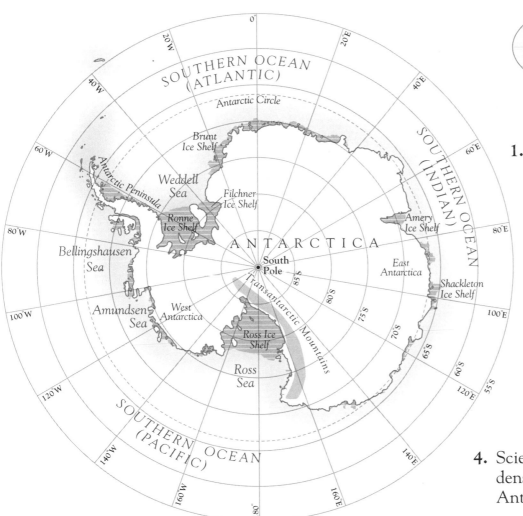

Key

Mountain range

Ice shelf

1. Antarctica is one of the driest / wettest places on the Earth.

2. The word "Antarctica" means "the opposite of the Arctic / Atlantic."

3. The Ross / Amery Ice Shelf lies between 160°E and 160°W.

4. Scientists found evidence of a dense forest / amusement park on Antarctica 100 million years ago.

5. The first explorers to reach the South Pole arrived in the 16th / 20th century.

★ Regions: The Mediterranean

FACTS

Some regions have an importance that goes beyond their physical size or population. One of these areas is around the Mediterranean Sea. This large body of water borders 20 countries and touches three continents—Asia, Africa, and Europe. As far back as 5,000 years ago, influential early civilizations, such as those of ancient Egypt, Rome, and Carthage, flourished around the Mediterranean Sea. The Mediterranean Sea continues to link the countries around it through trade and travel.

The Mediterranean region is made up of a number of smaller bodies of water in addition to the Mediterranean Sea. Look at the map and complete the sentences.

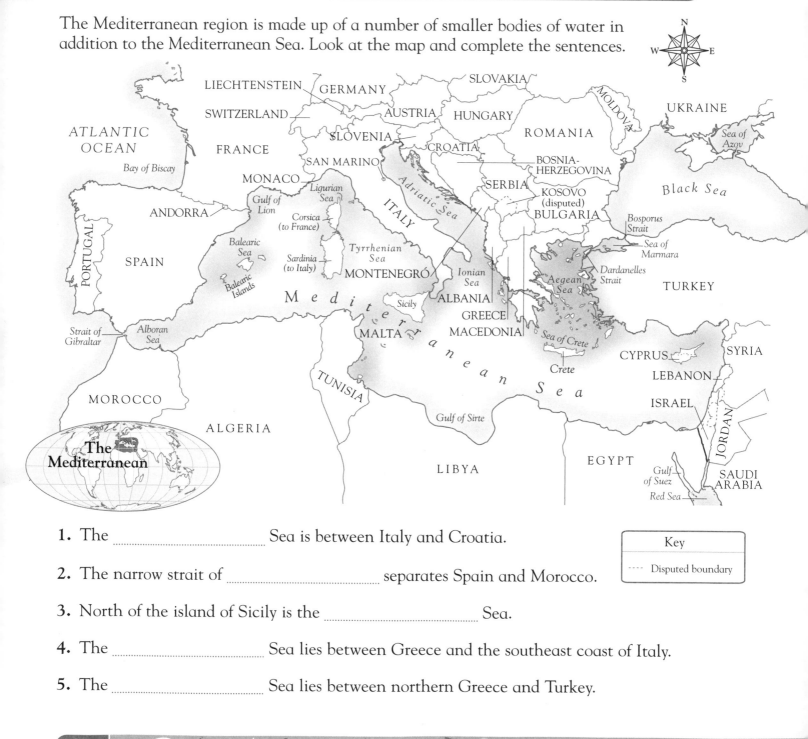

1. The _____ Sea is between Italy and Croatia.

2. The narrow strait of _____ separates Spain and Morocco.

3. North of the island of Sicily is the _____ Sea.

4. The _____ Sea lies between Greece and the southeast coast of Italy.

5. The _____ Sea lies between northern Greece and Turkey.

Key

----- Disputed boundary

The Middle East is a region without clearly defined borders. Its location is usually considered to be where Europe, Asia, and Africa come together. The Middle East was home to some of the earliest known civilizations, and Christianity, Islam, and Judaism began here. Today, this region is the main center for the production of petroleum and gas in the world. It is also frequently in the news for its political conflicts.

Look at this political map of the Middle East and neighboring northeast Africa. Then answer the questions.

Black Sea

★ Ankara

TURKEY

CYPRUS
Nicosia

Mediterranean Sea

LEBANON ★
Beirut

SYRIA
★ Damascus

★ Tehran

IRAQ

Baghdad ★

Caspian Sea

IRAN

Cairo ★

JORDAN
Amman

KUWAIT
Kuwait City

ISRAEL
Jerusalem

★

QATAR
Doha

EGYPT

BAHRAIN
Manuma

Persian Gulf

OMAN

Nile River

SAUDI
ARABIA

★ Riyadh

★

Gulf of Oman

UNITED ARAB
EMIRATES
Abu Dhabi

Muscat ★

OMAN

Red Sea

Arabian Peninsula

Arabian Sea

SUDAN
Khartoum ★

ERITREA
Asmara ★

YEMEN

Sana ★

*Socotra
(to Yemen)*

DJIBOUTI
Djibouti ★

Gulf of Aden

SOMALIA

Key

- - - Disputed boundary

★ Country capital

▨ Lake

The Middle East

1. Name the small nation on Iraq's southern border.

2. Which body of water separates Egypt from the Arabian Peninsula?

3. Which two countries border Saudi Arabia on the south?

4. Name the three largest countries (by size) in the Middle East.

5. Name the five countries that share a border with Syria.

The world map went through a huge change when the communist Soviet Union—a giant country made up of many nations—collapsed in 1991. The nations are now independent countries, and they include Belarus and Ukraine, the Baltic Sea countries of Lithuania, Latvia, and Estonia, and central Asian nations such as Kazakhstan, Uzbekistan, and Tajikistan. Even after the breakup of the Soviet Union, Russia remains the largest country in the world.

This map shows Russia, the former Soviet Union, and some countries of Eastern Europe. Use the map to unscramble the country names and then write their capital cities.

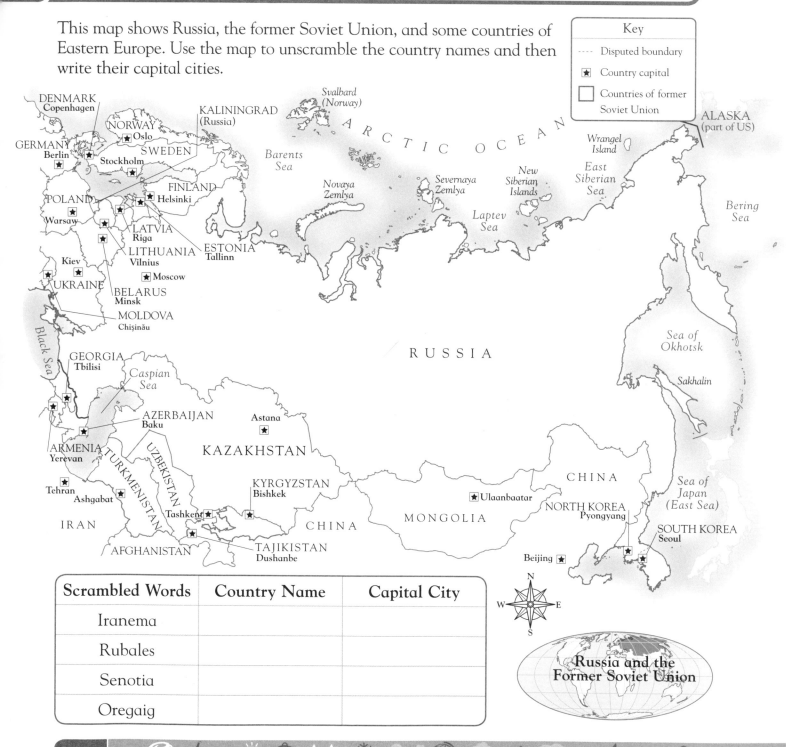

Key	
- - - -	Disputed boundary
★	Country capital
☐	Countries of former Soviet Union

Russia and the Former Soviet Union

Scrambled Words	Country Name	Capital City
Iranema		
Rubales		
Senotia		
Oregaig		

India is the seventh-largest country in the world, and second in population, after China. It is located on a "subcontinent"—a landmass smaller than a continent but very large. India is a huge peninsula that extends south into the Indian Ocean. It shares the subcontinent with other smaller countries, such as Pakistan and Nepal.

Study this map of the Indian subcontinent and answer the following questions.

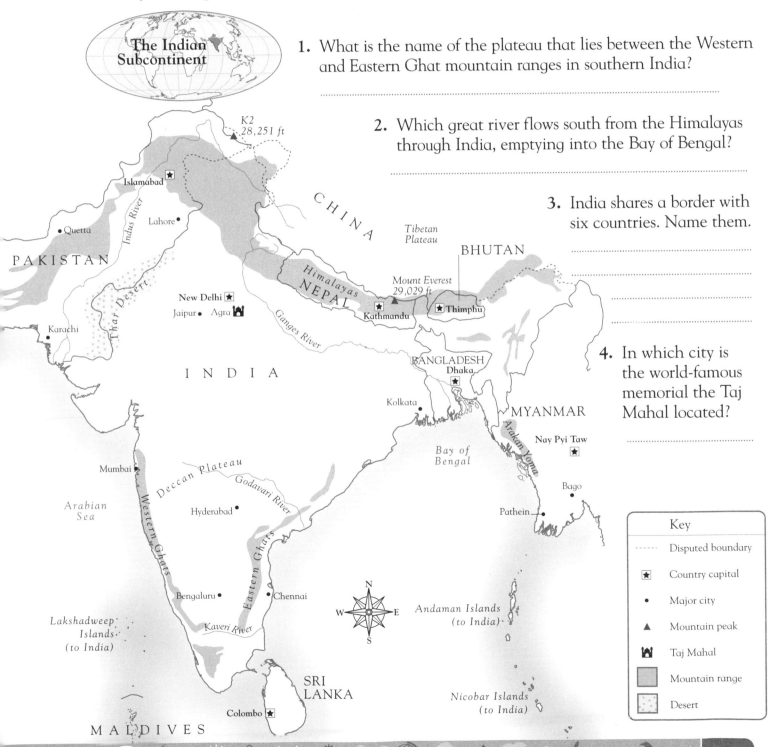

1. What is the name of the plateau that lies between the Western and Eastern Ghat mountain ranges in southern India?

....

2. Which great river flows south from the Himalayas through India, emptying into the Bay of Bengal?

....

3. India shares a border with six countries. Name them.

....

....

....

4. In which city is the world-famous memorial the Taj Mahal located?

....

Key

----- Disputed boundary

★ Country capital

• Major city

▲ Mountain peak

Taj Mahal

Mountain range

Desert

FACTS

East and Southeast Asia are home to approximately one out of every four people on Earth. China, a huge country with an enormous population, is the biggest nation in the region. The Chinese civilization dates back more than 4,000 years. After the US, China has the second-largest economy in the world, followed by Japan.

Imagine that you are about to take a journey around East and Southeast Asia. Look at this map to answer the questions and then draw the route you have taken.

1. Your trip begins in Manila, the capital of .... Your next stop is Phnom Penh, the capital of ....

2. After Phnom Penh, you will take a ship up the .... River. This will lead you to Vientiane in ....

3. Next, you fly to Ulaanbaatar, the capital of the landlocked nation of

   ....

4. Two days later, you will fly to your last destination, Seoul, which is the capital city of ....

Key

----- Disputed boundary

★ Country capital

〰 Lake

46

Geography and Earth's Future

In the 21st century, the world faces many difficult questions: How can we preserve our rain forests? What to do about Earth's rising temperatures? Why are some African lands becoming drier and less productive? With Earth's population at a record 7 billion and growing, how can all people be fed? A study of geography will help us understand how the Earth changed in the past, how it is changing today, what these changes might mean for the future, and how we can all work together to protect the Earth.

What would you do to preserve and protect the Earth? Take a look at this list of some 21st century challenges and pick one of them. Research and consider solutions that may help address the issue. Write them on the lines given below.

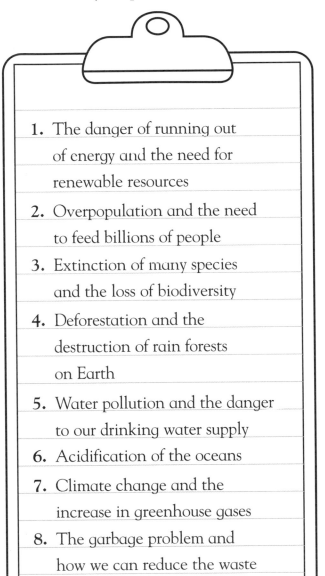

1. The danger of running out of energy and the need for renewable resources
2. Overpopulation and the need to feed billions of people
3. Extinction of many species and the loss of biodiversity
4. Deforestation and the destruction of rain forests on Earth
5. Water pollution and the danger to our drinking water supply
6. Acidification of the oceans
7. Climate change and the increase in greenhouse gases
8. The garbage problem and how we can reduce the waste we produce

Why does the problem exist?

....
....
....
....
....
....

Have people faced a similar problem in the past?

....
....
....
....
....
....

What solutions have been suggested?

....
....
....
....
....

Certificate

6th Grade

Congratulations to

....

for successfully finishing this book.

GOOD JOB!

You're a star.

Date

....

Answer Section
with Parents' Notes

This book is intended to support the geography concepts that are taught to your child in the sixth grade. It includes activities that test your child's knowledge of the world. By working through this book, your child will be able to learn basic geography concepts in a fun and informative way.

Contents

These activities are intended to be completed by a child with adult support. The topics covered are as follows:

- Natural world and the world built by humans;
- Maps and globes;
- Map projections;
- Hemispheres;
- Oceans;
- Latitude and longitude;
- Time zones around the world;
- Informational maps—population, rainfall, and natural resources;
- Physical features—mountains, rivers, deserts, rain forests, and biomes;
- Continents and countries;
- Important regions of the world.

How to Help Your Child

As you work through the pages with your child, make sure to explain what each activity requires. Read the facts and instructions aloud. Encourage questions and reinforce observations that will build confidence and increase active participation in classes at school.

By working with your child, you will understand how he or she thinks and learns. When appropriate, use props and objects from daily life to help your child make connections with the world outside.

If an activity seems too challenging, encourage your child to try another page. Give encouragement by praising your child's progress as he or she gives a correct answer and completes an activity. Good luck, and remember to have fun!

⭐ Understanding Earth

Humans have always wanted to understand the world in which they live. Geography is one way to understand our world. Geography comes from the Greek words "Geo," which means "Earth," and "graphia," which means "writing." It is the study of Earth's physical features and how these features affect our lives. It tells us about the location and features of the places on Earth. Geography presents a picture of where we live. In a way, geography is a guidebook to life on Earth.

How well do you know your home planet, Earth? Read the statements below and check (✓) if each one is **true** or **false**. Read carefully, since some of these are tricky!

1. Most of the Earth's surface is covered in water.

   True ✓   False ☐

2. The Earth always rotates from west to east.

   True ✓   False ☐

3. North America is located below the equator.

   True ☐   False ✓

4. Globes show the Earth more accurately than flat maps.

   True ✓   False ☐

5. It takes the Earth 24 hours to revolve around the sun.

   True ☐   False ✓

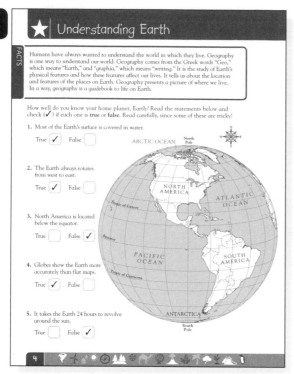

Discuss with your child the idea of geography as "a guidebook to life on Earth." Ask how a knowledge of geography might help people live better lives. Encourage your child to think about the kind of information that can be had from learning more about geography.

Our World ⭐

The surface of Earth is covered with many landforms and bodies of water—mountains and valleys, rain forests and deserts, rivers and oceans. Many of these natural features have been on our planet for millions of years. Over the past several thousand years, human beings have also built many important features on Earth to make life easier.

This map of part of the United States (US) shows some of its features—lakes, rivers, mountain peaks, cities, bridges, and highways. Look at the chart below. Put a check (✓) under **natural** or **built by humans** depending on the feature.

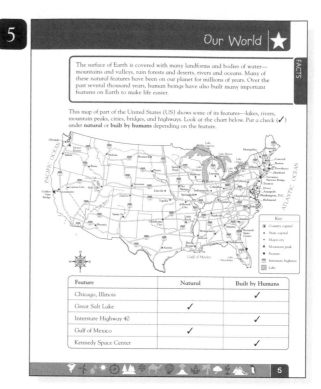

Feature	Natural	Built by Humans
Chicago, Illinois		✓
Great Salt Lake	✓	
Interstate Highway 40		✓
Gulf of Mexico	✓	
Kennedy Space Center		✓

Discuss the differences between the natural world and the world built by humans. Talk about how the natural world affects the built world and is, in turn, affected by what humans build. Discuss the built and natural landmarks in your community.

⭐ Maps and Directions

Maps are pictures that explain where places are in relation to each other. Maps help us to move from one place to another. They also describe how far one place is from another. Maps use directions to tell us where places are located. Mapmakers offer simple tools that help users make sense of maps.

Read the descriptions of the tools below and find them on this map of a city.

Compass Rose: Most maps have a tool called a compass rose. It shows the four directions—north, south, east, and west. The compass rose tells you which direction the top of the map is pointing toward.

Scale: Maps are pictures of very large places, and every map is smaller than the place it shows. The scale of a map tells you the distance an inch on a map represents, such as one mile or 1,000 miles.

Key or Legend: Maps use symbols to communicate information. These symbols, along with their explanations, are included in boxes on maps. These boxes are called keys or legends.

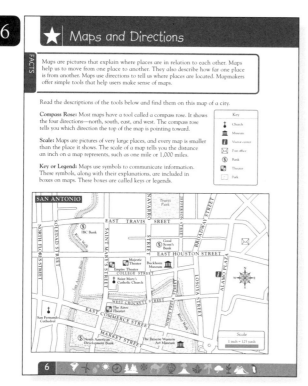

Find a map of your town, city, or county and talk to your child about how you use it. Ask if he or she has used a map to help get somewhere. Talk about how electronic maps and Global Positioning System (GPS) are changing the way people use, and depend on, maps.

Globes: Our Planet in 3-D ⭐

Flat maps do a good job of showing places on Earth. However, the best way to see things on the Earth is by putting a map on a rounded object—a globe. Flat maps have an advantage over globes: they are smaller and allow you to see everything at once. To see something on the other side of a globe, you must turn it. This may seem inconvenient, however, it is important because the Earth itself never stops spinning. Earth is tilted toward the sun and turns on an axis—an imaginary line that runs through the North Pole and South Pole. Flat maps do not spin, but globes do. This explains why a globe is the best way to represent Earth. It is shaped like our planet!

Take a look at the globe and the flat map pictured below. Fill in the chart by putting a check (✓) next to the one—**map** or **globe**—that shows the feature better.

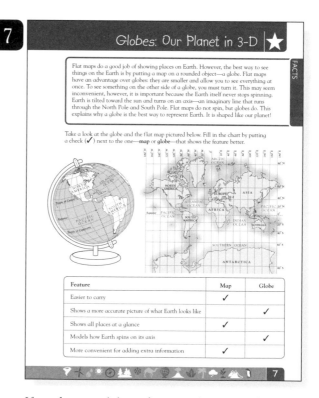

Feature	Map	Globe
Easier to carry	✓	
Shows a more accurate picture of what Earth looks like		✓
Shows all places at a glance	✓	
Models how Earth spins on its axis		✓
More convenient for adding extra information	✓	

If you have a globe at home, refer to it with your child and compare its features to those on a world map. Read the information on this page together, and then ask your child to come up with some more ways in which globes differ from maps.

★ Map Projections

FACTS

Globes are the best way to represent the spherical shape of the Earth, but flat maps are more convenient. The representation of a round Earth on a flat map is called a projection. While making projections, mapmakers have to distort the shape and size of the land in some ways. There are many types of projections. Here are two of them:
Mercator projection: This projection is good for showing directions, but distances and size of lands away from the equator are distorted.
Interrupted projection: Shapes and sizes of land are accurate on this projection, but distance and directions are distorted.

Look at the Mercator and Interrupted map projections and then answer the questions.

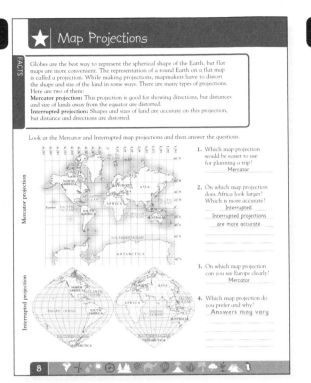

1. Which map projection would be easier to use for planning a trip?
   Mercator

2. On which map projection does Africa look larger? Which is more accurate?
   Interrupted.
   Interrupted projections are more accurate.

3. On which map projection can you see Europe clearly?
   Mercator

4. Which map projection do you prefer and why?
   Answers may vary

Explain the challenges in showing a round world on a flat map. To illustrate the many interesting ways in which our planet can be reproduced on flat maps, do an Internet search together for images of map projections.

Hemispheres ★

FACTS

We can divide the Earth into halves by using two imaginary lines. Each half is called a hemisphere, meaning "half of a round object." The equator is the imaginary line around the middle of the Earth that divides it into the northern hemisphere and the southern hemisphere. The prime meridian is the imaginary line running vertically from the North Pole to the South Pole. The area east of the prime meridian is the eastern hemisphere and the area west of it is the western hemisphere.

The maps show the four hemispheres. Look at the maps and then check (✔) the hemispheres in which the continents appear. **Note:** Some continents may fall in all four hemispheres.

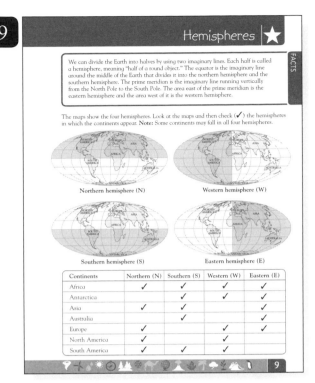

Northern hemisphere (N) Western hemisphere (W)

Southern hemisphere (S) Eastern hemisphere (E)

Continents	Northern (N)	Southern (S)	Western (W)	Eastern (E)
Africa	✔	✔	✔	✔
Antarctica		✔	✔	✔
Asia	✔	✔		✔
Australia		✔		✔
Europe	✔		✔	✔
North America	✔		✔	
South America	✔	✔	✔	

Invite your child to explore the question, "Why don't we have East and West poles?" Explain that because the Earth spins on its axis, which is an imaginary line that runs through the center of the Earth from the North Pole to the South Pole, our planet has an equator and is easily divided into North and South hemispheres.

★ Oceans

FACTS

More than two-thirds of Earth's surface is covered by water. The five oceans are the biggest bodies of water on Earth. The Pacific Ocean is the largest ocean, followed by the Atlantic, the Indian, the Southern, and the Arctic oceans. The Pacific is so large that you could fit all of Earth's land inside it! The saltwater oceans contain about 96 percent of all the water on Earth. All other bodies of water, such as rivers, lakes, and ponds, make up only four percent.

Study this map showing the oceans on Earth. Then answer the questions below.

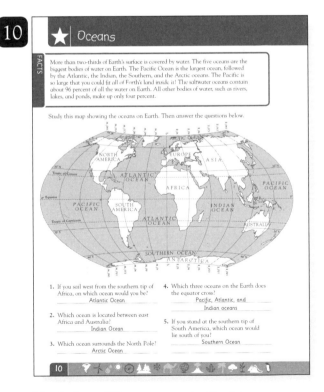

1. If you sail west from the southern tip of Africa, on which ocean would you be?
   Atlantic Ocean

2. Which ocean is located between east Africa and Australia?
   Indian Ocean

3. Which ocean surrounds the North Pole?
   Arctic Ocean

4. Which three oceans on the Earth does the equator cross?
   Pacific, Atlantic, and Indian oceans

5. If you stand at the southern tip of South America, which ocean would lie south of you?
   Southern Ocean

Until about 500 years ago, the Earth's oceans were major barriers to exploration. Encourage your child to think why that may have been the case. While on this topic, talk about the unknown distances, the crude state of ship technology, and how being days out of sight of land generated fear in sailors.

Continents ★

FACTS

The Earth is divided into seven large masses of land known as continents. Asia is the largest of the seven continents, followed by Africa, North America, South America, Antarctica, Europe, and Australia. Scientists estimate that two-thirds of all land is in the northern hemisphere and one-third is in the southern hemisphere. Scientists believe that the continents were once a big, connected landmass called Pangaea. This supercontinent was located in the middle of a super ocean.

Study this map of Earth's seven continents. Then answer the questions below.

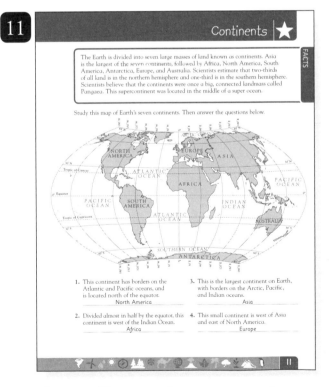

1. This continent has borders on the Atlantic and Pacific oceans, and is located north of the equator.
   North America

2. Divided almost in half by the equator, this continent is west of the Indian Ocean.
   Africa

3. This is the largest continent on Earth, with borders on the Arctic, Pacific, and Indian oceans.
   Asia

4. This small continent is west of Asia and east of North America.
   Europe

The story of Pangaea—the supercontinent that scientists believe once existed and connected all the continents—is fascinating to children. Assist your child in researching what it looked like. Then explore with him or her the evidence for Pangaea by piecing together today's continents.

★ Latitude

FACTS

The Earth is huge, so it can be difficult to give a precise location for any place on the planet. To address that problem, a grid with imaginary crisscrossing lines is used on globes and maps. The places where the lines meet are assigned numbers, providing an exact location. The imaginary, parallel, horizontal lines that run from east to west are known as latitudes. They are measured in degrees north and south. The imaginary horizontal line found at 0°, midway between the North Pole and the South Pole, is known as the equator. All other latitude lines are north or south of the equator. So, the North Pole is 90° north of the equator and the South Pole is 90° south. Lines in between are at 1° to 89° north or south.

Look at this map of some US cities. Use the latitudes to answer the questions.

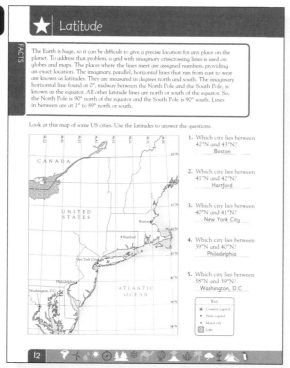

1. Which city lies between 42°N and 43°N?
   Boston

2. Which city lies between 41°N and 42°N?
   Hartford

3. Which city lies between 40°N and 41°N?
   New York City

4. Which city lies between 39°N and 40°N?
   Philadelphia

5. Which city lies between 38°N and 39°N?
   Washington, D.C.

Key
- Country capital
- State capital
- Major city
- Lake

Help your child find latitude 23.5°N on a world map. Explain that this is the Tropic of Cancer—the latitude line where the sun is directly overhead once a year around June 21. Ask him or her to find the southern hemisphere's equivalent line, the Tropic of Capricorn, which is at 23.5°S.

Longitude ★

FACTS

Longitudes are imaginary lines that run from north to south across the Earth, meeting at the North Pole and South Pole. The 0° line is the prime meridian. Longitudes are measured in degrees east and west.

This map shows North America with its longitudes and latitudes. Look at the map and answer the questions.

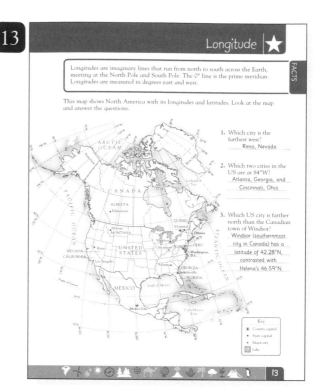

1. Which city is the furthest west?
   Reno, Nevada

2. Which two cities in the US are at 84°W?
   Atlanta, Georgia, and Cincinnati, Ohio

3. Which US city is further north than the Canadian town of Windsor?
   Windsor (southernmost city in Canada) has a latitude of 42.28°N, contrasted with Helena's 46.59°N

Key
- Country capital
- State capital
- Major city
- Lake

Ask your child to find out the latitude and longitude at which your home is located. Provide a map of your town or area to get a rough estimate. If possible, search for the exact coordinates of your house on the Internet.

★ Time Zones Around the World

FACTS

The Earth is always spinning on its axis. As the Earth turns, one-half points toward the sun (daytime) and the other half points away (nighttime). It takes the Earth 24 hours to complete one spin. To calculate the time in other parts of the world, time zones were created. Time zones are 24 vertical slices of the Earth.

On this time-zone map, it is 12 PM in London, England; Lisbon, Portugal; and Casablanca, Morocco. In the next zone to the east—which includes Paris, France, and Lagos, Nigeria—it is 1 PM. If you look at the United States, you will see that it is 7 AM in Washington, D.C., as well as in Lima, Peru. Look at the map carefully and figure out the time in places around the world.

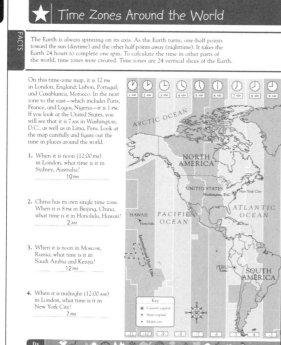

1. When it is noon (12:00 PM) in London, what time is it in Sydney, Australia?
   10 PM

2. China has its own single time zone. When it is 8 PM in Beijing, China, what time is it in Honolulu, Hawaii?
   2 AM

3. When it is noon in Moscow, Russia, what time is it in Saudi Arabia and Kenya?
   12 PM

4. When it is midnight (12:00 AM) in London, what time is it in New York City?
   7 PM

Key
- Country capital
- State capital
- Major city

Find a globe, or a ball of any size. Turn the globe, or the ball, to demonstrate the Earth's rotation. Use a flashlight to show how sunlight reaches different parts of the Earth at different times. Then use the time zone map on the activity page to discuss the time differences between your country to that of other places on Earth.

Time Zones Around the World ★

FACTS

These imaginary slices run from the North Pole to the South Pole. Each time zone represents one hour. Since the Earth rotates from west to east, the time in every zone is one hour later than the next zone to the west. A few large countries—including India and China—have created their own time zones.

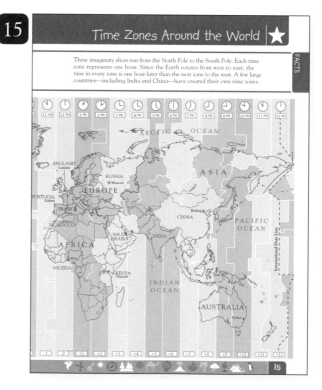

Flying has changed human beings' relationship to time. If you have ever taken a plane to a country in a different time zone, tell your child about how that affected your trip. You can discuss if you had to adjust your watch, or if you suffered from jet lag. Tell your child how moving from east to west differs from moving from west to east in terms of time.

★ Informational Maps: Introduction

FACTS Informational maps present data about a town, a city, a state, a country, or a continent. These maps use symbols and colors to show facts about an area's climate, population, foods grown, etc. Each map creates a picture of an aspect of life.

This map shows which side of the road people drive on in each country. Study the map and answer the questions below.

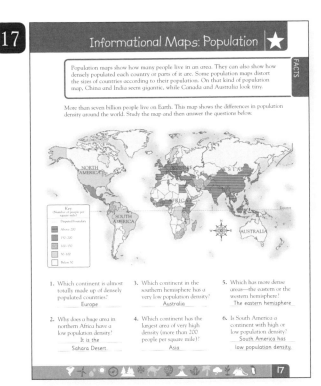

1. Every continent shown here has at least one country where people drive on the left side of the road. In North America, they are the island nations of Jamaica and the Bahamas. Which letter shows the location of the Bahamas? **C**

2. India, Pakistan, and Bangladesh border each other in the Indian subcontinent and all drive on the left side of the road. Which letter shows their location? **B**

3. One continent allows driving only on the left side of the road. Which letter shows that continent? **F**

4. Does your country follow the left-side or right-side driving rule? Do all the countries in your continent follow the same rule?

   Answers may vary

Discuss how informational maps turn facts into pictures and symbols. Ask: "What makes an informational map helpful?" Then turn to the map on the activity page and discuss how this map would be useful to someone driving from India to Europe.

Informational Maps: Population ★

FACTS Population maps show how many people live in an area. They can also show how densely populated each country or parts of it are. Some population maps distort the sizes of countries according to their population. On that kind of population map, China and India seem gigantic, while Canada and Australia look tiny.

More than seven billion people live on Earth. This map shows the differences in population density around the world. Study the map and then answer the questions below.

Key (Number of people per square mile)
- Disputed boundary
- Above 200
- 150–200
- 100–150
- 50–100
- Below 50

1. Which continent is almost totally made up of densely populated countries?
   Europe

2. Why does a huge area in northern Africa have a low population density?
   It is the
   Sahara Desert.

3. Which continent in the southern hemisphere has a very low population density?
   Australia

4. Which continent has the largest area of very high density (more than 200 people per square mile)?
   Asia

5. Which has more dense areas—the eastern or western hemisphere?
   The eastern hemisphere

6. Is South America a continent with high or low population density?
   South America has
   low population density.

Explain how population density affects people's lives by talking about the density in your town. Ask questions: "How often do we get stuck in traffic?" or, "Do you see crowds frequently?" To exhibit differing densities, show the streetscape of New York City and that of a small town on the Internet.

★ Informational Maps: Rainfall

FACTS Rain falls just about everywhere on Earth, but in different amounts. The amount of rain affects what grows and lives in an area. Areas that receive more than 80 inches of average rainfall a year have dense rain forests. Areas that receive fewer than 10 inches of rain per year are considered deserts.

This map shows four different levels of annual rainfall around the world. Study the map and then circle the letter corresponding to the correct answer in the questions below.

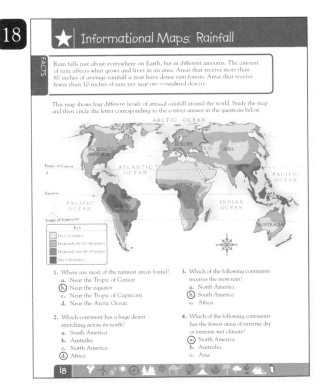

Key
- Dry (+10 inches)
- Moderately dry (10–40 inches)
- Moderately wet (40–80 inches)
- Wet (+80 inches)

1. Where are most of the rainiest areas found?
   a. Near the Tropic of Cancer
   b. Near the equator
   c. Near the Tropic of Capricorn
   d. Near the Arctic Ocean

2. Which continent has a huge desert stretching across its north?
   a. South America
   b. Australia
   c. North America
   d. Africa

3. Which of the following continents receives the most rain?
   a. North America
   b. South America
   c. Africa

4. Which of the following continents has the fewest areas of extreme dry or extreme wet climate?
   a. North America
   b. Australia
   c. Asia

The map on this activity page shows the places on Earth where water is plentiful and where it is not. Ask your child to think about rainfall in relation to your town, the seasons of the year, and even sporting events. Then ask, "How are these things affected by the amount of rainfall we receive?"

Informational Maps: Natural Resources ★

FACTS Natural resources are valuable materials from the Earth, such as gold, oil, and wood. Some resources, such as coal, can be used only once, and are nonrenewable, while other resources, such as water and wind, are called renewable resources. Special maps show where these resources can be found so countries can make good use of them.

In the US, wind is being used to create energy for power supplies. This map shows the average annual strengths of wind across the US. Study the map and then circle the correct answers.

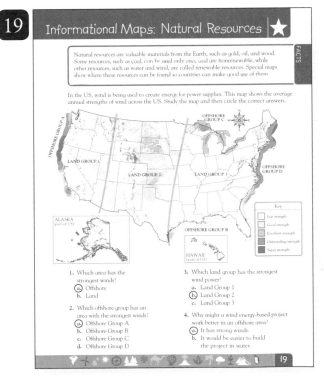

Key
- Fair strength
- Good strength
- Excellent strength
- Outstanding strength
- Super strength

1. Which area has the strongest winds?
   a. Offshore
   b. Land

2. Which offshore group has an area with the strongest winds?
   a. Offshore Group A
   b. Offshore Group B
   c. Offshore Group C
   d. Offshore Group D

3. Which land group has the strongest wind power?
   a. Land Group 1
   b. Land Group 2
   c. Land Group 3

4. Why might a wind energy-based project work better in an offshore area?
   a. It has strong winds.
   b. It would be easier to build the project in water.

To discuss the importance of conservation, teach your child about the value of preserving natural resources. Ask: "How can you help?" While discussing this, talk about clean air, water, healthy soil, and the importance of conserving nonrenewable resources, such as petroleum or coal.

★ Physical Features: Introduction

FACTS

Earth is covered with physical features, such as mountains, plains, plateaus, deserts, rivers, lakes, and forests. The physical features of a place affect the ways people use the land. For example, some flatlands with rich soil could be suitable for growing crops, whereas other flatlands are better for raising livestock.

The United States has many major physical features. This map shows some of those features. Use the map to identify the features mentioned in the descriptions below.

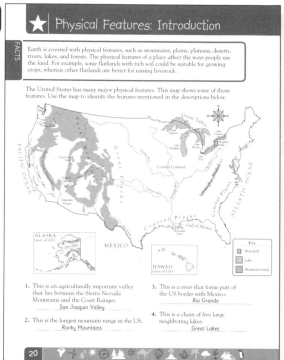

1. This is an agriculturally important valley that lies between the Sierra Nevada Mountains and the Coast Ranges.
   San Joaquin Valley

2. This is the longest mountain range in the US.
   Rocky Mountains

3. This is a river that forms part of the US border with Mexico.
   Rio Grande

4. This is a chain of five large neighboring lakes.
   Great Lakes

Ask your child why understanding the physical features of an area is important. While talking about Earth's features, give meaningful examples, such as, people planning a new city need to know if the river that runs nearby can be used by ships all year long or if it floods often.

Physical Features: Mountains ★

FACTS

Mountains are landforms that rise from the Earth to a height far above the surrounding land. While some mountains are very steep, others slope up gradually. Mountains are found on all the seven continents. A few stand alone, but many are part of mountain ranges.

"The Seven Summits" is the name given to the highest mountain peaks on the seven continents. Read the descriptions of the peaks below. On the map, write the number that matches their location.

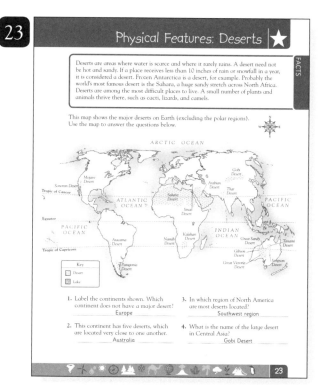

1. The world's highest peak, Mount Everest, is located in Asia. It is 29,029 ft high.
2. Located in the Andes in South America, Mount Aconcagua is 22,831 ft tall.
3. Denali, also called Mount McKinley, is North America's highest peak, at 20,310 ft.
4. Mount Kilimanjaro is the highest peak in Africa, at 19,341 ft.
5. Mount Elbrus of the Caucasus range in Europe is 18,510 ft high.
6. Antarctica's highest peak is the Vinson Massif. It is 16,050 ft high.
7. Mount Kosciuszko is Australia's highest peak, at 7,310 ft.

With your child, review the list of Earth's highest mountain peaks on this activity page. "What is it about peaks that makes people want to climb them?" Have your child research the Guinness World Records to find out interesting facts about Earth's biggest, longest, and coldest peaks.

★ Physical Features: Rivers

FACTS

Rivers are large flowing bodies of water found all over the world. They are usually, though not always, freshwater. Rivers were very important to early humans, providing food, drinking water, a place to wash, and a way to travel long distances. Rivers remain vital to life on Earth today. Some rivers are enormous. For example, the Amazon River in South America and the Nile River in Africa are both more than 4,000 miles long.

This map shows the 10 longest rivers that flow through the United States. Locate them on the map and find the names in the wordsearch below.

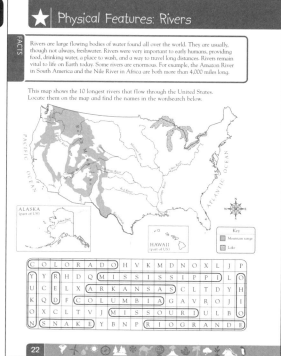

Explore the concept of "continental divide." Explain that all rivers flow into other bodies of water, and that every continent has a divider, such as a mountain range, that sends rivers east or west, north or south. Then with your child, research the continental divides in the US.

Physical Features: Deserts ★

FACTS

Deserts are areas where water is scarce and where it rarely rains. A desert need not be hot and sandy. If an area receives less than 10 inches of rain or snowfall in a year, it is considered a desert. Frozen Antarctica is a desert, for example. Probably the world's most famous desert is the Sahara, a huge sandy stretch across North Africa. Deserts are among the most difficult places to live. A small number of plants and animals thrive there, such as cacti, lizards, and camels.

This map shows the major deserts on Earth (excluding the polar regions). Use the map to answer the questions below.

1. Label the continents shown. Which continent does not have a major desert?
   Europe

2. This continent has five deserts, which are located very close to one another.
   Australia

3. In which region of North America are most deserts located?
   Southwest region

4. What is the name of the large desert in Central Asia?
   Gobi Desert

Discuss how deserts are difficult places to live, given the little rain and resources. Talk about the plants and animals that thrive there, such as cacti, camels, and tortoises. Encourage your child to find out facts about the few groups of people who make homes in Earth's deserts.

★ Physical Features: Rain Forests

Rain forests are wet areas with dense vegetation. They cover only two percent of the Earth's surface, but half of all animal and plant species are found in them. The three largest rain forests are the Amazon in South America, the Congo Basin in Africa, and the Southeast Asian rain forest. Rain forests are extremely important to life on Earth, but humans are tearing down parts of them. Scientists warn that we need to preserve rain forests and protect the creatures living in them to keep our planet healthy.

Most rain forests are divided vertically into four very different layers. They are **forest floor**, **understory**, **canopy**, and **emergent**. Look at this picture of a rain forest below. Read the descriptions and identify each layer. First, write the name of the layer on the picture. Then write the number of the layer next to its correct description.

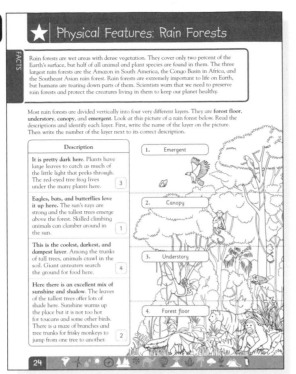

Description	
It is pretty dark here. Plants have large leaves to catch as much of the little light that peeks through. The red-eyed tree frog lives under the many plants here.	3
Eagles, bats, and butterflies love it up here. The sun's rays are strong and the tallest trees emerge above the forest. Skilled climbing animals can clamber around in the sun.	1
This is the coolest, darkest, and dampest layer. Among the trunks of tall trees, animals crawl in the soil. Giant anteaters search the ground for food here.	4
Here there is an excellent mix of sunshine and shadow. The leaves of the tallest trees offer lots of shade here. Sunshine warms up the place but it is not too hot for toucans and some other birds. There is a maze of branches and tree trunks for frisky monkeys to jump from one tree to another.	2

1. Emergent
2. Canopy
3. Understory
4. Forest floor

Rain forests are not only home to remarkable animal and plant life, but they also provide ingredients for many medicines. However, humans are rapidly tearing down rain forests for development projects. Discuss the trade-offs between conservation and development.

Physical Features: Biomes ★

A biome is an area with distinct vegetation, climate, and animal life. Types of biomes include forests, deserts, grasslands, and tundra. Biomes can be further divided. For example, all deserts get little rain, but there are hot deserts, such as the Sahara; warm, semiarid deserts, such as the Great Basin Desert in the US; cool, coastal deserts, such as the Atacama in Chile; and cold polar deserts, such as Antarctica. Animals that thrive in one biome are unlikely to survive in others.

There are three major types of forest biome. Read the chart and answer the questions below.

Name of Biome	Description	Where Found	Animals Found
Tropical (Rain forest)	Warm and rainy all year. Little light filters down to the floor of these dense, dark forests. This biome is greatly endangered.	In warm climates, often near the equator, in North America, South America, Africa, Australia, and Asia	Tropical birds, bats, insects, and small mammals
Temperate (Deciduous)	Warm in summer, cold in winter, and rainy all year. In summer, broadleaf trees let some sunlight reach the forest floor. In colder months, leaves fall off trees.	Moderate climate areas of North and South America, northeastern Asia, and Western and Central Europe	Squirrels, deer, rabbits, skunks, bears, wolves, mountain lions, bald eagles, and bobcats
Boreal (Taiga)	Evergreen forests with short, wet, warm summers and long, dry, cold winters. Thick, dense trees with needles instead of leaves prevent much light from reaching the forest floor.	Cold northern areas of Eurasia and North America, including Siberia, Alaska, northern Canada, and Scandinavian countries	Moose, bears, weasels, foxes, wolves, deer, bald eagles, and hawks

1. Which type of forest goes through the most dramatic change in appearance over the course of a year? How does it change?
   Temperate forest. The trees lose their leaves in winter.

2. One of these biomes is not found in the southern hemisphere. Which one is it?
   Boreal

3. Which continent is not listed on this chart?
   Antarctica

4. Which biome has the least amount of rainfall?
   Boreal

5. In which biome will you find moose?
   Boreal

Take a walk around your community with your child and ask, "What kinds of mini-environments can you find nearby?" Encourage him or her to come up with terms like forests, riverbanks, urban areas, parkland, etc. Discuss the animals and plants that thrive in these areas.

★ North America: Physical Features

North America is Earth's third-largest continent. It is located in the northern and western hemispheres and has everything from glaciers to rain forests. North America's climate changes radically from north to south. Alaska, parts of northern Canada, and Greenland have very cold winters. The middle regions are mostly temperate and the southern regions are tropical.

Study this map of North America showing some of its physical features. Find the letter on the map that matches the descriptions given below, then write the letter next to the description.

1. The Colorado River flows through the Sonoran Desert — B
2. The "land bridge" of Central America to South America — D
3. The Rocky Mountains — A
4. Canada's enormous Hudson Bay — E
5. The Yucatán peninsula, in southern Mexico — F
6. The five Great Lakes between the US and Canada — C

Since many people think of North America as comprising only the US, Canada, and Mexico, facts on this page may surprise your child. Explain that Central America is also included in this continent. Ask your child if any other facts about North America were surprising.

North America: Political Divisions ★

North America is made up of three very large countries—the United States, Canada, and Mexico. The continent also includes the smaller countries of Central America, such as Panama, Guatemala, and Costa Rica, and the island nations of the Caribbean, such as Dominican Republic, Cuba, Jamaica, and Haiti. Greenland, the world's largest island, is also a part of North America. However, it is a territory of the European country of Denmark.

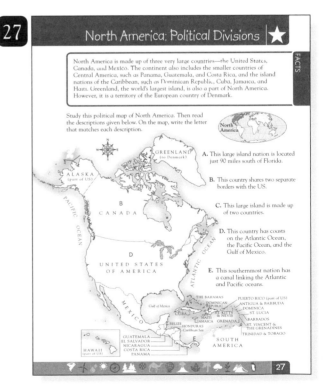

Study this political map of North America. Then read the descriptions given below. On the map, write the letter that matches each description.

A. This large island nation is located just 90 miles south of Florida.

B. This country shares two separate borders with the US.

C. This large island is made up of two countries.

D. This country has coasts on the Atlantic Ocean, the Pacific Ocean, and the Gulf of Mexico.

E. This southernmost nation has a canal linking the Atlantic and Pacific oceans.

Canada, the world's second-largest country, is one of the most sparsely populated nations on Earth. Provide a map of Canada and help your child consider why its population is just one-tenth of the US's population. Discuss how climate can affect population density.

★ United States: States and Population

The United States of America, stretching from the Atlantic Ocean to the Pacific Ocean, is home to more than 300 million people. It has 50 states, 48 of which are contiguous (connected). The other two states are Alaska, bordering Canada in the far north, and Hawaii, a series of islands in the Pacific Ocean.

The total population of the United States, according to the 2010 Census, was 308,745,538. This map is based on the 2010 Census and shows the differences in population across the 50 states. Use the map to answer the questions below.

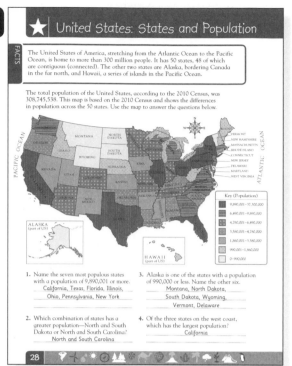

Key (Population)
- 9,890,001–37,500,000
- 6,490,001–9,890,000
- 4,780,001–6,490,000
- 3,580,001–4,780,000
- 1,860,001–3,580,000
- 990,001–1,860,000
- 0–990,000

1. Name the seven most populous states with a population of 9,890,001 or more.
   California, Texas, Florida, Illinois, Ohio, Pennsylvania, New York

2. Which combination of states has a greater population—North and South Dakota or North and South Carolina?
   North and South Carolina

3. Alaska is one of the states with a population of 990,000 or less. Name the other six.
   Montana, North Dakota, South Dakota, Wyoming, Vermont, Delaware

4. Of the three states on the west coast, which has the largest population?
   California

Use this activity page to explore the idea of what defines a nation. Explain that most countries are composed of contiguous, or connected land. However, in the US, Alaska and Hawaii are separated from the mainland by many miles. Discuss what makes them part of the US.

United States: Capital Cities ★

Capital cities are places where the branches of government are located. The capital of the United States is Washington, D.C., but each of the 50 states also has a capital. Sometimes, the capital is the largest city in the state—for example, Atlanta, Georgia. However, for most states in the US, the capital is a less populous city. For example, the capital of New York State is not New York City, with its eight million residents, but Albany, with a population below 150,000.

This map shows the capital cities of the 48 contiguous states in the US. Use the map to answer the questions below.

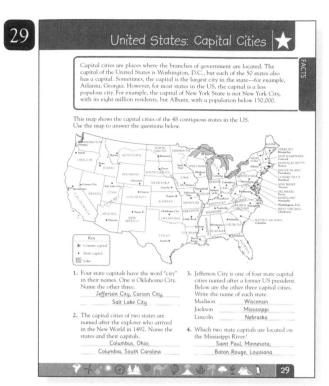

Key
- ◉ Country capital
- • State capital
- Lake

1. Four state capitals have the word "city" in their names. One is Oklahoma City. Name the other three.
   Jefferson City, Carson City, Salt Lake City

2. The capital cities of two states are named after the explorer who arrived in the New World in 1492. Name the states and their capitals.
   Columbus, Ohio; Columbia, South Carolina

3. Jefferson City is one of four state capital cities named after a former US president. Below are the other three capital cities. Write the name of each state.
   Madison — Wisconsin
   Jackson — Mississippi
   Lincoln — Nebraska

4. Which two state capitals are located on the Mississippi River?
   Saint Paul, Minnesota; Baton Rouge, Louisiana

Explain to your child that almost every US state capital has a capitol, but these two terms are not the same. The capitol is the building where a state's lawmakers sit, while the capital is the city in which they meet. Use the Internet to show photos of capitol buildings in the US.

★ United States: Alaska and Hawaii

Alaska and Hawaii became the 49th and 50th states of the US, respectively, in 1959. They are the only two US states separated by land or water from the other 48. Located near the Arctic Circle, Alaska is the largest US state and has a cold climate most of the year. Hawaii is a series of small islands in the Pacific Ocean and has a warm climate all year.

Study these maps of Alaska and Hawaii. Then answer the questions below.

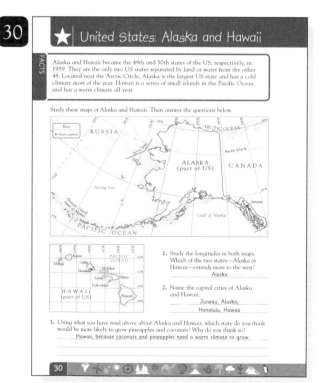

Key
- • State capital

1. Study the longitudes in both maps. Which of the two states—Alaska or Hawaii—extends more to the west?
   Alaska

2. Name the capital cities of Alaska and Hawaii.
   Juneau, Alaska; Honolulu, Hawaii

3. Using what you have read above about Alaska and Hawaii, which state do you think would be more likely to grow pineapples and coconuts? Why do you think so?
   Hawaii, because coconuts and pineapples need a warm climate to grow.

The technique of comparing and contrasting is a valuable academic skill. Help your child strengthen this skill by asking him or her to find the differences and similarities between Alaska and Hawaii. Ask: "How are they different?" (by size, population, climate) and "How are they similar?" (separated from mainland; have many islands, etc.).

United States: Time Zones ★

The United States is a large country, and it crosses six time zones. In the 48 contiguous states, there are four time zones. Therefore, when it is 9 AM in the Eastern Time Zone, it will be 8 AM in the Central Time Zone, 7 AM in the Mountain Time Zone, and 6 AM in the Pacific Time Zone. As for the other two states, it will be 5 AM in Alaska, which is in the Alaskan Time Zone, and, in standard time, 4 AM in Hawaii, which is located in the Hawaii-Aleutian Time Zone.

Study this map of the US showing the different time zones. For each city, a time has been given. Write what the time will be in Denver, Colorado. **Note:** Use the map on p.14 to help you.

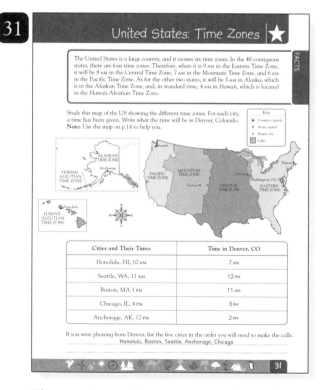

Key
- ◉ Country capital
- • State capital
- ◼ Major city
- Lake

Cities and Their Times	Time in Denver, CO
Honolulu, HI, 10 AM	7 AM
Seattle, WA, 11 AM	12 PM
Boston, MA 1 PM	11 AM
Chicago, IL, 4 PM	3 PM
Anchorage, AK, 12 PM	2 PM

If you were phoning from Denver, list the five cities in the order you will need to make the calls.
Honolulu, Boston, Seattle, Anchorage, Chicago

The exercise on this activity page asks students to calculate the time differences across some cities in the US. If you have family in other parts of the country, ask your child to calculate the time difference in those states. Together, figure out the time differences for you calling those relatives, and for them calling you.

★ South America: Physical Features

FACTS

South America is Earth's fourth-largest continent. It is located in the northern, southern, and western hemispheres. At its north lies the Caribbean Sea. To its west is the Pacific Ocean, and to its east is the Atlantic Ocean. South America has varied physical features and a diverse climate. It has the Earth's largest rain forest—the Amazon; one of Earth's driest places—the Atacama Desert; and Earth's longest mountain range—the Andes.

Study this map of South America showing some of its physical features. Find the letter on the map that matches the descriptions given below and write the letter next to the description.

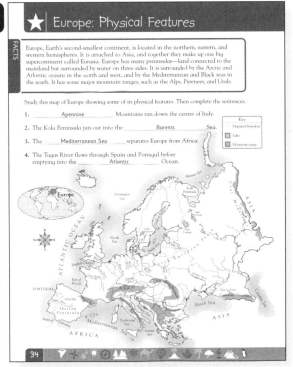

1. The Andes Mountains travel down the western side of the continent. **C**

2. The Atacama Desert is west of the Andes and is 600 miles long. **E**

3. The tropical Amazon Rain Forest surrounds the Amazon River. **A**

4. The Guiana Highlands is a forested plateau in the northern part of South America. **F**

5. The Pampas are low-lying flatlands in the south of South America. **B**

6. Patagonia is the southernmost region of South America. **D**

South America embodies Earth's remarkable diversity. Here, one of Earth's wettest places, the Amazon Rain Forest, is located only a few hundred miles from Earth's driest place, the Atacama Desert. Encourage your child to name other contrasting environments on Earth, such as the tropics and the poles.

South America: Political Divisions ★

FACTS

South America is home to countries of varied sizes—large ones such as Brazil, Peru, and Argentina, and smaller ones such as Suriname, Guyana, and Uruguay. Until the 1800s, most South American countries were controlled by Spain, while Brazil was ruled by Portugal. At present, South America has 12 independent countries. The regions of French Guiana and the Falkland Islands are parts of France and the United Kingdom, respectively. South America has many well-developed large cities, such as Santiago, Lima, Buenos Aires, Sao Paulo, Rio de Janeiro, and Bogotá.

Study this political map of South America and write the name of the country that matches each description.

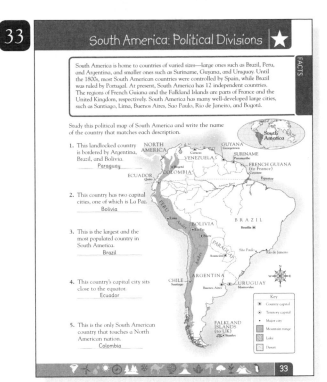

1. This landlocked country is bordered by Argentina, Brazil, and Bolivia. **Paraguay**

2. This country has two capital cities, one of which is La Paz. **Bolivia**

3. This is the largest and the most populated country in South America. **Brazil**

4. This country's capital city sits close to the equator. **Ecuador**

5. This is the only South American country that touches a North American nation. **Colombia**

In our increasingly connected global world, children should know more about the world outside the US. Ask your your child to research one of the 12 South American nations, and then to tell you about its population, land, and history. Talk about similarities between the US and that country.

★ Europe: Physical Features

FACTS

Europe, Earth's second-smallest continent, is located in the northern, eastern, and western hemispheres. It is attached to Asia, and together they make up one big supercontinent called Eurasia. Europe has many peninsulas—land connected to the mainland but surrounded by water on three sides. It is surrounded by the Arctic and Atlantic oceans in the north and west, and by the Mediterranean and Black seas in the south. It has some major mountain ranges, such as the Alps, Pyrenees, and Urals.

Study this map of Europe showing some of its physical features. Then complete the sentences.

1. __Apennine__ Mountains run down the center of Italy.

2. The Kola Peninsula juts out into the __Barents__ Sea.

3. The __Mediterranean Sea__ separates Europe from Africa.

4. The Tagus River flows through Spain and Portugal before emptying into the __Atlantic__ Ocean.

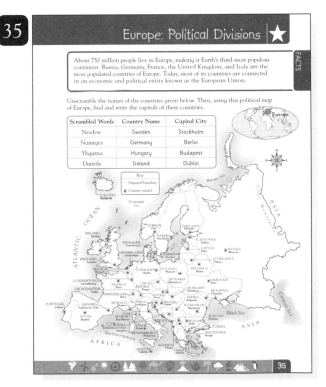

Europe's geography is crucial to its peoples' daily lives. Explore with your child how Europe's key mountain chain, the Alps, is a climate dividing line that affects the climate of regions around it: To the mountains' north, weather is often rainy and cold, and to the south, it's often sunnier and warmer.

Europe: Political Divisions ★

FACTS

About 750 million people live in Europe, making it Earth's third-most populous continent. Russia, Germany, France, the United Kingdom, and Italy are the most populated countries of Europe. Today, most of its countries are connected in an economic and political entity known as the European Union.

Unscramble the names of the countries given below. Then, using this political map of Europe, find and write the capitals of these countries.

Scrambled Words	Country Name	Capital City
Nesdew	Sweden	Stockholm
Namrgey	Germany	Berlin
Yhgurna	Hungary	Budapest
Danrile	Ireland	Dublin

Europe is a great example of historical change. It was the center of World Wars I and II. Although it is a relatively wealthy and peaceful continent, in recent years, it has been subject to turmoil. Using recent news reports, discuss with your child some current events of this continent.

★ Asia: Physical and Political

FACTS

Asia is the largest continent on Earth. It is located in the northern and eastern hemispheres. Although it is on the same landmass as Europe, Asia is separated from Europe by the Ural Mountains and the Caspian Sea. This continent is home to the world's tallest mountain chain—the Himalayas; Earth's lowest point—the Dead Sea; and Earth's highest plateau—the Tibetan Plateau. It has a large desert, the Gobi, and vast rivers—Ganges in India, Huang He in China, and Mekong in Vietnam. More than 4.3 billion people reside in Asia. This is more than half of the world's population. The world's most populous countries, China and India, are located in Asia.

Study this map of Asia showing its physical features and political divisions. Then fill in the answers in the crossword puzzle on the following page.

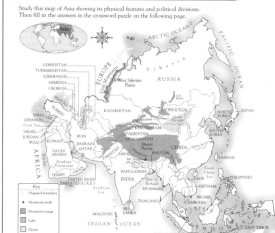

Look at the maps of Asia and Europe with your child. Point out how the two are really one landmass, with the Ural Mountains and Caspian Sea creating a kind of dividing line. Tell your child to research the reasons as to why the landmass is considered two continents.

Asia: Physical and Political ★

Read the descriptions of some of Asia's important physical features and political divisions. Then, using the map on the previous page, complete the crossword.

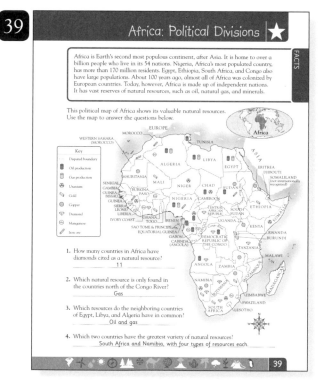

Across

1. A river that forms part of the border between Laos and Thailand
2. A major river that flows through Iraq
3. The Earth's highest and biggest plateau, located in Central Asia
4. A major river that flows through India
5. An ocean surrounding Asia on the east
6. A large desert that stretches across Mongolia and China
7. An ocean north of Russia

Down

1. A cluster of small islands in the Indian Ocean, southwest of Sri Lanka
2. Earth's second most populous nation, located south of the Himalayas
3. The northernmost region of Asia, which has a very cold climate
4. A landlocked country between Russia in the north and China in the south
5. An island country located some miles off the southeast coast of China
6. A landlocked lake, called a "sea," forming part of Kazakhstan's border

Together with your child, find out about Asia—Earth's most populous continent—and its changing economies, especially those of China and India. Ask your child to list some important facts about Asia, and then discuss what its new economic status may mean for the rest of the world.

★ Africa: Physical Features

FACTS

Africa is the second-largest continent on Earth. It extends over the four hemispheres. It is bordered by the Mediterranean Sea in the north, the Red Sea and the Indian Ocean in the east, and the Atlantic Ocean in the west. Africa is home to the world's largest desert—the Sahara; the world's longest river—the Nile; one of the world's biggest waterfalls—Victoria Falls; and the world's second-largest rain forest—Congo Basin. Africa's remarkable wildlife includes camels, gorillas, giraffes, elephants, and lions.

Read the descriptions of some of Africa's physical features below. On the map, write the number at the location that matches each description.

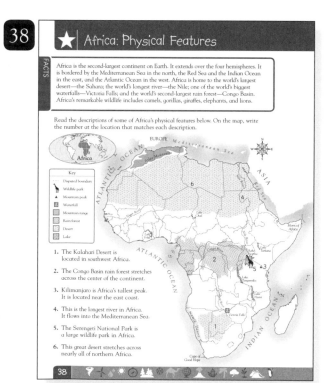

1. The Kalahari Desert is located in southwest Africa.

2. The Congo Basin rain forest stretches across the center of the continent.

3. Kilimanjaro is Africa's tallest peak. It is located near the east coast.

4. This is the longest river in Africa. It flows into the Mediterranean Sea.

5. The Serengeti National Park is a large wildlife park in Africa.

6. This great desert stretches across nearly all of northern Africa.

Africa is full of remarkable geographical features and unusual plant and animal life. This activity page discusses some of the continent's famed natural landmarks. Assist your child in researching the story of any one of these marvels—Nile River, Kalahari Desert, Mount Kilimanjaro, Serengeti Park, etc.

Africa: Political Divisions ★

FACTS

Africa is Earth's second most populous continent, after Asia. It is home to over a billion people who live in its 54 nations. Nigeria, Africa's most populated country, has more than 170 million residents. Egypt, Ethiopia, South Africa, and Congo also have large populations. About 100 years ago, almost all of Africa was colonized by European countries. Today, however, Africa is made up of independent nations. It has vast reserves of natural resources, such as oil, natural gas, and minerals.

This political map of Africa shows its valuable natural resources. Use the map to answer the questions below.

1. How many countries in Africa have diamonds cited as a natural resource?
   11

2. Which natural resource is only found in the countries north of the Congo River?
   Gas

3. Which resources do the neighboring countries of Egypt, Libya, and Algeria have in common?
   Oil and gas

4. Which two countries have the greatest variety of natural resources?
   South Africa and Namibia, with four types of resources each.

More than 100 years ago, most of Africa was ruled by European nations. Today, the continent is made up of more than 50 independent countries. In 2011, a new African nation was born—South Sudan. Ask your child to find the location of this new country using the map on the activity page.

★ Australia

FACTS

Australia is the smallest of all continents on Earth. It is nicknamed "the land down under" because it is the only inhabited continent that does not extend above the equator. Australia is also the only continent made up of just one country, and the only one that is an island, not touching any other landmass. Australia is bordered by the Indian Ocean on the west and the Pacific Ocean on the east.

Look at this map showing Australia's provinces and natural features. Read the descriptions below and write the name of the location.

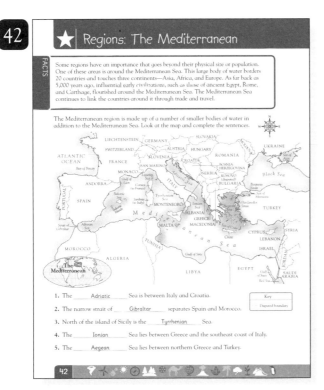

1. A spectacular underwater attraction off the coast of Queensland
   Great Barrier Reef

2. The Australian State that is a separate island
   Tasmania

3. Australia's northernmost city, named after a scientist
   Darwin

4. A major city on the west coast of Australia
   Perth

5. A huge sandstone rock located in the Northern Territory
   Uluru, or Ayers Rock

Children are fascinated by Australia's unusual wildlife, which includes kangaroos, koalas, and platypuses. Ask: "Why is Australia home to strange creatures?" Explain that Australia's isolated location is a major factor. Use the Internet to search for more unusual animals.

Antarctica ★

FACTS

Antarctica is the frozen continent surrounding the South Pole. It is the fifth-largest continent (bigger only than Europe and Australia). About 98 percent of Antarctica is covered with a thick sheet of ice all year. It gets very, very cold there. In July 1983, the temperature at Vostok Research Station went down to −128.6 °F (−89.2 °C). It was the lowest temperature ever recorded on Earth. The only people living on Antarctica are involved in scientific study.

Here are some facts about Antarctica. Cross out the wrong word from the two options given to make the fact correct.

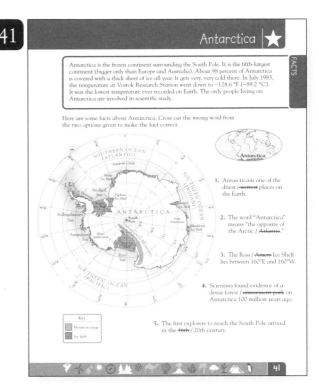

1. Antarctica is one of the driest / ~~wettest~~ places on the Earth.

2. The word "Antarctica" means "the opposite of the Arctic / ~~Atlantic~~."

3. The Ross / ~~Amery~~ Ice Shelf lies between 160°E and 160°W.

4. Scientists found evidence of a dense forest / ~~amusement park~~ on Antarctica 100 million years ago.

5. The first explorers to reach the South Pole arrived in the ~~16th~~ / 20th century.

Antarctica is the only continent on Earth that does not have any countries; it is an international zone. It is also the last continent to be explored. Assist your child in finding out more about Antarctica, especially the remarkable story of Roald Amundsen and Robert Scott's race to the South Pole.

★ Regions: The Mediterranean

FACTS

Some regions have an importance that goes beyond their physical size or population. One of these areas is around the Mediterranean Sea. This large body of water borders 20 countries and touches three continents—Asia, Africa, and Europe. As far back as 5,000 years ago, influential early civilizations, such as those of ancient Egypt, Rome, and Carthage, flourished around the Mediterranean Sea. The Mediterranean Sea continues to link the countries around it through trade and travel.

The Mediterranean region is made up of a number of smaller bodies of water in addition to the Mediterranean Sea. Look at the map and complete the sentences.

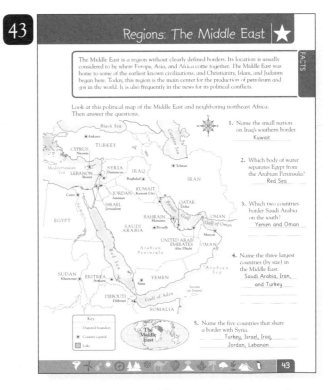

1. The **Adriatic** Sea is between Italy and Croatia.

2. The narrow strait of **Gibraltar** separates Spain and Morocco.

3. North of the island of Sicily is the **Tyrrhenian** Sea.

4. The **Ionian** Sea lies between Greece and the southeast coast of Italy.

5. The **Aegean** Sea lies between northern Greece and Turkey.

The next few activity pages in this workbook cover the crucial regions of today's world. This page shows the Mediterranean region, which was the site of important civilizations, such as ancient Egypt, and the Greek and Roman empires. Explore with your child how the Mediterranean Sea links this region in trade, travel, and migration even today.

Regions: The Middle East ★

FACTS

The Middle East is a region without clearly defined borders. Its location is usually considered to be where Europe, Asia, and Africa come together. The Middle East was home to some of the earliest known civilizations, and Christianity, Islam, and Judaism began here. Today, this region is the main center for the production of petroleum and gas in the world. It is also frequently in the news for its political conflicts.

Look at this political map of the Middle East and neighboring northeast Africa. Then answer the questions.

1. Name the small nation on Iraq's southern border.
   Kuwait

2. Which body of water separates Egypt from the Arabian Peninsula?
   Red Sea

3. Which two countries border Saudi Arabia on the south?
   Yemen and Oman

4. Name the three largest countries (by size) in the Middle East.
   Saudi Arabia, Iran, and Turkey

5. Name the five countries that share a border with Syria.
   Turkey, Israel, Iraq, Jordan, Lebanon

The region of the Middle East is a hot spot of religious, political, and human rights unrest. Explain to your child that the borders of many of these nations were established only some 100 years ago. To help your child better understand this region, suggest that he or she select one of these countries and research its 20th century history.

★ Regions: Russia and the Former Soviet Union

The world map went through a huge change when the communist Soviet Union—a giant country made up of many nations—collapsed in 1991. The nations are now independent countries, and they include Belarus and Ukraine, the Baltic Sea countries of Lithuania, Latvia, and Estonia, and central Asian nations such as Kazakhstan, Uzbekistan, and Tajikistan. Even after the breakup of the Soviet Union, Russia remains the largest country in the world.

This map shows Russia, the former Soviet Union, and some countries of Eastern Europe. Use the map to unscramble the country names and then write their capital cities.

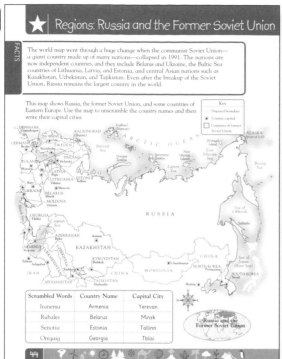

Scrambled Words	Country Name	Capital City
Irunema	Armenia	Yerevan
Rubales	Belarus	Minsk
Senotia	Estonia	Tallinn
Oregaig	Georgia	Tblisi

Discuss how Russia remains an important world power today, even though the Soviet Union is now only a historical name. Explain how empires, world politics, and even maps are ever-changing, even in our own time.

Regions: The Indian Subcontinent ★

India is the seventh-largest country in the world, and second in population, after China. It is located on a "subcontinent"—a landmass smaller than a continent but very large. India is a huge peninsula that extends south into the Indian Ocean. It shares the subcontinent with other smaller countries, such as Pakistan and Nepal.

Study this map of the Indian subcontinent and answer the following questions.

1. What is the name of the plateau that lies between the Western and Eastern Ghat mountain ranges in southern India?
   Deccan Plateau

2. Which great river flows south from the Himalayas through India, emptying into the Bay of Bengal?
   Ganges

3. India shares a border with six countries. Name them.
   Pakistan, China, Nepal, Bhutan, Bangladesh, and Myanmar

4. In which city is the world-famous memorial the Taj Mahal located?
   Agra

Talk to your child about India's growing economic power, which has brought focus to this region. Explain that India is part of a complex area because it shares the subcontinent with Pakistan and Bangladesh. Ask your child to research the languages in these countries; more than 100 languages are spoken in India alone.

★ Regions: East and Southeast Asia

East and Southeast Asia are home to approximately one out of every four people on Earth. China, a huge country with an enormous population, is the biggest nation in the region. The Chinese civilization dates back more than 4,000 years. After the US, China has the second-largest economy in the world, followed by Japan.

Imagine that you are about to take a journey around East and Southeast Asia. Look at this map to answer the questions and then draw the route you have taken.

1. Your trip begins in Manila, the capital of Philippines. Your next stop is Phnom Penh, the capital of Cambodia.

2. After Phnom Penh, you will take a ship up the Mekong River. This will lead you to Vientiane in Laos.

3. Next, you fly to Ulaanbaatar, the capital of the landlocked nation of Mongolia.

4. Two days later, you will fly to your last destination, Seoul, which is the capital city of South Korea.

The region of China and Southeast Asia is an area of remarkable history, architecture, and natural beauty. With your child, look up each of the cities mentioned in this activity page. The astonishing variety in this crucial region will be of great interest.

Geography and Earth's Future ★

In the 21st century, the world faces many difficult questions: How can we preserve our rain forests? What to do about Earth's rising temperatures? Why are some African lands becoming drier and less productive? With Earth's population at a record 7 billion and growing, how can all people be fed? A study of geography will help us understand how the Earth changed in the past, how it is changing today, what these changes might mean for the future, and how we can all work together to protect the Earth.

What would you do to preserve and protect the Earth? Take a look at this list of some 21st century challenges and pick one of them. Research and consider solutions that may help address the issue. Write them on the lines given below.

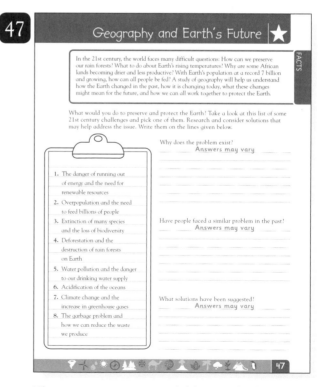

1. The danger of running out of energy and the need for renewable resources
2. Overpopulation and the need to feed billions of people
3. Extinction of many species and the loss of biodiversity
4. Deforestation and the destruction of rain forests on Earth
5. Water pollution and the danger to our drinking water supply
6. Acidification of the oceans
7. Climate change and the increase in greenhouse gases
8. The garbage problem and how we can reduce the waste we produce

Why does the problem exist?
Answers may vary

Have people faced a similar problem in the past?
Answers may vary

What solutions have been suggested?
Answers may vary

This activity page invites children to think about Earth's most pressing problems. Use this activity to help your child develop research and thinking skills. Discuss these problems and suggest ways to research information about them. Then help your child come up with some solutions.